Advance Praise for

D ra:

A DAUGHTER OF UNFORGIVING TERRAIN

"Dora Rodriguez is the modern day hero we so desperately need. I was forever changed after reading her story of survival, love, and perseverance. A must read for these dark times."

— **Javier Zamora**
author of *Solito*

"Dora Rodriguez is a remarkable human being. Her story of survival and lifelong commitment to saving lives in the borderlands is an inspiration. Her memoir comes at a critical moment in history and should be read by everyone. We need more of Dora's compassion and empathy in the world."

— **Melissa del Bosque,**
co-founder of *The Border Chronicle*

"There are few people in this world who inspire me more than Dora Rodriguez—her story is the very embodiment of tenacity and resilience, of hope and solidarity. If you want to understand how the cruelty and violence of border enforcement might be transformed into the raw material for inspiration, grace, and service, look no further."

— **Francisco Cantú,**
author of *The Line Becomes a River*

"Some books speak straight to the soul, and this is one of them. Dora is a nuanced, heart-filled, and heartbreaking tale from one of the most committed, sagacious, and inspiring activists I've ever met. Tracing her multiple attempts at finding safety, a profound tragedy in the desert, and her own coming-of-age as a mother and activist, Rodriguez details the human costs of border militarization—and how she overcame them. This is a crucial book of crystalline moral clarity."

John Washington,
investigative reporter, translator, & author
The Dispossessed (2020)
The Case for Open Borders (2024)

In memory of all my friends who lost their lives seeking the safety of a better future, and who longed to be reunited with their loved ones. I am deeply sorry you never had the chance to hug them one last time. Please know that I have never forgotten you. Each of you will always live on in my heart.

In memory of all the children and people around the world who die every day seeking refuge from violence. No human being deserves to die in the pursuit of basic human rights.

¡Presente!

With profound gratitude to all the humanitarians who show up—day after day—to walk beside others on this journey.

Thank you for leading with compassion, for offering love instead of judgment, and for reminding us all of our shared humanity.

A DAUGHTER OF UNFORGIVING TERRAIN

———

ISBN: 978-1-967254-04-0 - *hardcover*
ISBN: 978-1-967254-05-7 - *softcover*
ISBN: 978-1-967254-06-4 - *e-book*

———

Credits

Cover Design / Trever Ducote
Back Cover Photography / Lisa Elmaleh
Book Design & Production / timmyroland.com

Dora:

A DAUGHTER OF UNFORGIVING TERRAIN

A MEMOIR BY

DORA RODRIGUEZ

RESILIENCIA
PUBLISHING

Content Warning

——

This book contains accounts and descriptions of sexual violence and trauma.

Contents

On my third and final trip,
we headed into the Sonoran Desert
as twenty-six.

Thirteen of us survived.

Chapter One

Organ Pipe Cactus
National Monument, Arizona, Spring 2024

"I heal in honor of my friends." I look at the young faces of the Northwestern University students brought to the border through a program offered by the Sheil Catholic Center. They stand beside the brightly painted crosses Alvaro had placed to honor those who didn't survive our journey. I think of my family and the volunteers who helped haul the concrete and rocks to this desolate location so that those who didn't survive could be honored. I take a deep breath and continue.

"I heal because, for some reason, I was chosen to live. There were three sisters in the group I left with: twelve, fourteen, and sixteen years old. I hadn't met them before the journey, but I became like a big sister to them. In the end, I couldn't keep them alive."

I flash back to being curled up in a ball under the little shade cast by a palo verde tree. I was exhausted, confused, and afraid I would die alone in the desert and no one would find my remains to send back to my mother. "In the end, I pretended to be dead so the smuggler wouldn't kill me too."

I can still hear the thirsty, weak voices of the women closest to the Salvadoran smuggler pleading with him to save them, but the smuggler was as delirious as we were, and there was no reasoning with him. In the end, he went completely mad.

I often wonder if I am reopening old wounds by coming

to this place every year. This desert wash has become sacred to me, and my annual visits feel like a continuation of my journey because I am able to remember and honor my friends.

I was the same age as these students when I crossed into the United States forty-three years ago. Nineteen is so young. Some of them weep. In all the conversations that take place about immigration, no one talks about forced migration, that many people have no choice and must leave with only a moment's notice.

I often ask groups to imagine getting a knock on their door, alerting them that a fire is nearby and they must evacuate immediately. What would they do? What would they take? This feeling of desperation and urgency is a reality for many who arrive at our borders. They are fleeing for their lives. Many of us have been forced from our homes and communities. It's essential that these students understand this.

"I aim to shine a light on those who feel invisible. Immigrants are people. I am a person. We all deserve to be seen, to live. No one deserves to die this way. We are seeking a better life, seeking safety from death in our own countries."

A dozen students are standing with their hands clasped in front of them. No one reaches out to comfort another. They are each in their own private place.

"I heal because of all of the humanitarians alongside me."

I look over at Sister Judy and see her move her lips in silent prayer. We have been doing this work beside each other for so many years now. I glance at Dorothy, a retired nurse who comes to the border to bandage the horribly wounded feet of migrants, to wrap their torn knees from the falls they take at night, to remove the cactus spines embedded in their skin.

"I had no idea what I was getting myself into when I left

my country. I only knew that if I stayed, I would be killed. You can't overthink such a decision. There is no way to measure the risk. You get up and do whatever needs to be done in the moment to try and save yourself."

My friend and fellow humanitarian James Holeman jumps in, "This was Dora's third attempt to cross."

I smile and nod. "The first two were brief. In January of 1980, I was arrested crossing into Tijuana and sent back to El Salvador. The entire trip took less than a week. I was still wearing the same clothes I had left in when I returned home," I say. A few students grin.

I think of my brown Levi corduroys. I had worked so hard to earn the money to pay for them for my high school graduation night. They were my most cherished pair. They fit my petite body perfectly. I would end up wearing them in each of my attempts to cross.

"On the second attempt, in April of the same year, I was arrested in Yuma, Arizona, and sent home again."

Such brief sentences don't even begin to touch on the gravity of those attempts or the extreme grief I felt leaving my mother, my family, and all my comforting and familiar routines.

Mi cultura. I left everything I knew behind.

Chapter Two

Roots of Resilience
Santa Ana, El Salvador, 1970s

I always had an organizing spirit and a passion for creating better places for people. I loved imagining new ways of doing things. I can't remember not being this way. My mom said that I was born with a liberation flag in my head because I was born on September 15, Independence Day in El Salvador. Perhaps that's it. Maybe it came from my grandmother, *Mamá* Lipa. She didn't have much, but she always shared what little she had. I learned from watching her.

She had many children of her own, yet somehow always made space in her heart and home for others. I remember sneaking a bit of laundry soap from my mother's house, tucking it into my backpack, and riding the bus after school to bring it to *Mamá* Lipa. We didn't even have enough ourselves, but I couldn't show up empty-handed. She had mentioned needing it, and I wanted to help in any way I could.

Even with so little, she always found a way to feed those who came to her door. It's her spirit I carry with me now.

Our neighborhood—*colonia*—consisted of the Catholic church, a single school, dozens of tiny houses, and a modest park that we had built ourselves. In the late seventies, my mother became part of a group similar to Habitat for Humanity here in the United States, led by one of the social work students. Our entire family joined in and helped organize our community to build homes in *La Matepec*, a

5

neighboring *colonia*.

My mother, grandfather, brothers Manuel and Oscar, and sister Mary would walk to *La Matepec* every Saturday to build a house for a family. We worked like ants, carrying more than our weight, piling mud, mixing it into a mash like oatmeal, latticing the *duralita* for the roof to keep out the sky. The days rushed by, and we accomplished so much. It indeed was a community effort.

Grandmothers made us food, young men hauled in supplies, and everyone helped where they could. We used materials from the earth and were steeped in faith. Whatever the earth gave us would be enough, and from this enduring faith, our community would build a better life. We raised walls, homes, schools, and churches, and we prepared meals. There was enough happiness and joy to be shared by all.

Along with the homes for others, we were building one for ourselves. We completed our own two-bedroom house with a private bathroom within a year. I can still hear the voice of the young social worker who was overseeing the entire project say, "*Señora* Maria Luisa, congratulations on owning your new home."

My mother's eyes filled with tears, and at the same time, a huge smile spread across her face. She hugged me and my siblings, and we all celebrated - we had done it! This was our safe home, a place of new beginnings and hope. We moved in as fast as we could. We did not own much, but we did have a bed and a small dining table. My mother rented a truck to help us move our few belongings.

My Aunt Rosa, who was my grandfather's younger sister, also lived with us. *Tía* Rosa was a caring, loving, and powerful woman. She had a black cat that was her baby, as she had never had children of her own. The night we moved to our new *casita*, she got a pillowcase and stuck the crying cat into it so it could not see the way to our new place. *Tía* Rosa believed that if the cat could see the way, it would escape and return to our old home. I imagined the cat gathering all its belongings and heading back to our old home in protest, and it made me laugh.

My father did not believe in education, especially for girls. He fought my mother when she told him that I was going to go to high school and would someday become a social worker. This made him so angry. I remember hiding behind the curtain, listening to her defend me, ready to jump out and save her if he became violent, which he often did. Shaking with fear and sadness, I heard my father repeatedly tell my mother, "She will become a whore, and it will be all your fault." My mother refused to give up the dream that I would finish high school and attend university someday.

My father left for the U.S. before we started our new house and never returned. He never sent the support back as he had promised once he was established in Arizona. I would later learn that he had continued to drink, married without divorcing my mother, and had another child. But, at this moment, my mother still held out hope that he would send the support that never came. Nevertheless, as a family, we managed to rise above it all and take care of ourselves.

I was the eldest of four children and took pride in being my mother's second-in-command. Before our new *casita*, we had a small, one-room house with a dirt floor and an *horno*—a mud stove where we cooked. We lived in this house until I was fifteen and my father left.

In El Salvador, it is typical to share a communal area with a patio and bathroom, known as a *mesón*. Each home faces the open patio where kids play and everyone gathers. This is also where we would haul in our water in buckets to shower.

We didn't have the luxury of dreaming about what we would eat each day. Instead, we needed to determine where the money would come from to buy the basics. My mother made tortillas for me to sell. Forty cents would be enough to buy dinner for our family of five.

Mamá Lipa would tell me, "Solutions will present themselves with a little creative thinking." I would care for another family's children or clean their house and get paid with a plate of food, taking the burden of one more mouth to feed away from my mother.

In El Salvador, there were no laws against child labor. It was necessary for children to contribute to their families' survival. From the time I was nine years old, my summer breaks were spent working in the coffee fields with *Mamá* Lipa, my two aunts, and dozens of other women from all over our country.

My aunts would joke that it was like a vacation, although we worked incredibly hard. We laughed, made good money, rarely saw any men, and had our meals consisting of a large corn tortilla and pinto beans. We basked in the little luxuries of these short months, not having to think about where our meals would come from and knowing exactly what each day would hold. We worked ourselves until our hands were black from the sweetness of the fruit and made jokes to keep each other laughing.

Sometimes, my Uncle Neto and Uncle Carlos would join us in the fields. They were so entertaining and full of energy. They made the days pass even faster. After a long day of picking beans, they would go hunting for *garrobos* or *cusucos* a few nights a week. They would return excited when they had a successful hunt, because that meant a meal with meat. They grew tired of eating tortillas and beans every night.

From our small town, we rode in the back of a truck together for hours, deep into the jungle where the coffee plants grew. The air got thicker under the dense forest canopy with each mile that we rode. The birds chattered loudly as we bounced around in the open truck bed, and I was so happy to be with these women. I lost track of days while we were together, picking coffee beans. Sometimes the rain would pour down on us, a warm shower that rinsed our sweat away, washed our clothes, and cleansed us for our next day's work. I had never been to a place without streets and buildings, but it was a place where I felt like I belonged.

Each day, we would start at 5:00 a.m., hiking up the mountain and then down a very steep hill with loose earth. I would carry a stick to try to balance myself. I had a basket tied around my waist and a sack slung around my back. Looking back, it was probably dangerous, but I saw it all as an adventure.

As I made my way through the aisles of towering plants, I would grab the largest coffee bean I could find and pop it into my mouth. The outside of the crimson husk was sweet, and the bean inside gave me enough energy to work until the trees were covered in shadows and my hands were stained with the sticky-sweet fruit. We were assigned to a row of plants, spending the day picking ruby red beans with their surprisingly bright green centers. I always hoped that my row would have enough ripe and ready scarlet beans, low enough for me to reach, so that I could make as much money as possible.

When dinner was ready, we retraced our morning steps, back up the mountain with the day's harvest balanced on our heads in baskets or carried on our backs in sacks. I reveled in the hot, damp days, sweating so much that my clothes never fully dried.

On one of the hottest afternoons I can remember in the fields, I felt something cool and damp trickle down my leg. I grabbed my thigh, thinking I would find a slug, but instead, my hand came away streaked in blood. I realized that it was the blood my aunts had told me about. Their stories had made it sound so intense, but now that it was here, it felt like a horrible mess and terrible timing.

I ran to find my *tías* and tell them what was happening, but I came across an old lady at the ranchero's house first. I told her I wasn't feeling well, and she asked me to sit down and then brought me a glass of lemonade. I was too embarrassed to tell her about my current situation, so I politely sat and drank the lemonade while blood soaked my pants and dripped onto the floor. When she walked back inside, I jumped up and ran as fast as I could to my aunts, telling them what I had done.

They listened and then burst out laughing. "Every woman knows about it, Dorita. It's no shame."

I waited and waited for the end of the day so my *Tío Neto* would come back from the coffee fields. He took me home on the bus to my mother. He stayed calm and told me not to worry, reassuring me that my mom wouldn't be upset that I had started my period.

Although we were the same age, I had always thought of my aunts as women but had never seen myself as one. I had felt like an adult for a long time, but the specific rules and responsibilities of womanhood were still lost on me.

That night, I slept under the stars and dreamed of a woman's life, maybe mine. I saw many babies. Then I thought of my mother raising us all alone. Maybe I wouldn't rush into this phase of life. Perhaps I would have only one child. I wanted to travel by boat and by plane. I wanted to see places I had never seen before, places I could barely describe. I imagined a vague, faraway world, and it brought me peace.

The harvest party at the end of the summer was the first time I had ever met people from all over El Salvador. I introduced myself to everyone, feeling energized with pride at the opportunity to work for my family. I showed the younger girls how to spot the best fruit on the coffee plants, even though most of it was already picked clean and loaded onto trucks bound for the cities by then.

Every year, this celebration was filled with longing and sadness, a mixture of homesickness colliding with the fear of never returning to this place that brought me happiness. It was an unshakable duality that stirred my heart and left me with a feeling of foreboding.

I returned from the coffee fields one summer to our new home in *La Matepec.* It marked a new chapter in my family's life. For the first time, we had our own bathroom, and my father would not be living with us.

Our new neighborhood had limited drinking water, so I would haul the laundry to the river on Saturday mornings to wash the clothes in the rocky basin. I would scrub and wring wet clothes for hours. My mother worked seven days a week at the hospital laundry, washing and ironing clothes by hand all day, and I didn't want her to come home and have to do the same for us. So I gave myself the task of being in charge of the family washing and ironing. I made many trips to the river and back, carrying *cantaritos* of water on my head for our daily use. It felt as though my days were filled with walking, walking, and more walking.

Service had become my passion from a young age. I attended Colegio San Lorenzo, a Catholic high school, where I was the queen of the soccer team, and after school, I led the Cub Scout boys, aged seven to ten. Each evening, I helped my mother run a food stand after her laundry job.

All this work never amounted to us owning a car, a bike, or even having enough money for the local bus. We didn't expect much compensation for our work. Service was our mission, and hope was our motivation. Finances were always challenging, and still, we remained a happy family. We hoped for an easier future, where we would always enjoy togetherness and happiness that no amount of money could buy.

Chapter Three

The Shift in El Salvador

In 1979, the social and political energies started shifting in the country. Leftist revolutionaries had been growing in power for years, and the increasingly militarized, conservative government responded by sending its military troops to every corner of the country, enforcing its rule and order. The troops were known as "death squads," *escuadrón de la muerte*, because they would regularly target union leaders, community organizers, and anyone they suspected of sympathizing with the revolutionaries. Our small *colonia, La Matepec,* on the outskirts of Santa Ana, became one of the most targeted areas.

It was a war against people with nothing to bargain with, low-income communities accused of being vulnerable to leftist ideologies. There was no middle class where we lived. Our *colonia* was small, a *familia*, and despite our efforts to protect it, poverty and desperation eventually made their way onto our streets. We were pushed beyond the limits of our control while civil unrest percolated throughout the country.

By the end of 1979, more and more kids were dropping out of school to sell drugs in nearby Santa Ana. Drugs attracted gangs and violence. Both attracted the military. Every family was affected, as stories spread like madness on the news. Mothers prayed for help, asking the government to save their families. Husbands, sons, and daughters were killed, and those who survived were left without any work. Food was scarce. These were the shared stories of hundreds of thousands of people throughout El Salvador.

Promotores were active during this time. These community health workers, *promotores de salud*, visited impoverished towns across the country, providing health education, resources, and support to underserved populations. They would organize and coordinate the construction of new homes in communities where people were existing on rations, living beneath cardboard ceilings, and lacking access to schools and medicine.

Once I graduated from high school at the end of 1979, I planned to study at the Universidad Santa Ana to become a *promotor*. Service was already my life's work, and the support of a university would allow me to travel to further places and create and implement systems that would outlive me.

My friend Carlos was a *promotor* who lived with his wife and two beautiful daughters in the house behind ours. One day, he left for what should have been a short journey to assist in a neighboring town and didn't return. A few days passed, and questions about him remained unanswered. A week later, his body was found buried among the underbrush at the edge of town.

Maxalino, another *promotor*, was tied to a tree at the entrance to the community. A crowd surrounded him, crying and screaming. He was mutilated, blackened from head to toe, burned with acid. I rushed home, letting others take care of his body. I couldn't be seen in those crowds without also becoming a target, but I will never forget how I last saw him.

The soldiers began regularly patrolling our neighborhoods, rifles strapped to their bodies, their faces covered. When they would knock on our doors, we didn't know if they had come to take someone away or were handing out propaganda for the government.

I was dating a boy from high school, Andres, who was considered to be in a higher social class than I was. He lived with his mom, who was a professor. His dad, fortunately, lived in the United States. While he had fears similar to mine, Andres had an easier way to leave El Salvador through his dad. It was nice having his companionship during such a dark and uncertain time.

Andres had given me a record, *Las Casas de Carton,* that the protesters would play loudly at every rally, but even he agreed that we should only play it quietly in my room. Through our thin walls, my mother would hear the unmistakable songs about our country's enduring pain.

> . . . *How sad, the rain is heard*
> *On the cardboard roofs.*
> *How sadly my people live*
> *In the cardboard houses.*
> *You're not going to believe,*
> *But there are schools for dogs,*
> *And they give them education*
> *So they don't bite the newsboys.*
> *But the boss, for years, many years,*
> *He is biting the worker. . . .*

"*Hija,*" she would call me, "Watch what you say, watch where you go. People are watching you."

"*Mamá,*" I'd say, "I haven't done anything wrong. I'm not afraid."

"Dora, they are taking people who are not guilty of anything."

The next day, soldiers marched down our street in huge numbers. Eighty soldiers in rows of twenty, going to every house to search for anti-government propaganda. With their rifles pointed at our neighbor's door, I yelled to my younger brother, "Oscar! *¡Ay Dios!* Break that record!" With eyes full of fear, Oscar froze in the hallway with the record in his hands. I pulled it from his clenched fists, smashed the vinyl into tiny pieces, and threw them into the outhouse just as the officers used their rifles to pound on our door.

Chapter Four

The Last Dance of Youth

We planned our graduation party as if joy itself could keep the soldiers away. Even with fear settling into our days, we held tight to the small moments that reminded us we were still young, still dreaming. It was a fragile kind of hope, but in those days, even the smallest hope felt like resistance.

My high school senior class sold bread, tortillas, and *pupusas*, held raffles, and performed plays to raise $100 for our graduation party. We rented a venue—*un salón de fiesta* —and chairs, bought *panes con pollo*, and a white sheet cake that said *Clase de Noviembre 1979*. My good friends Maritza, Consuelo, and I decorated the room. We made brightly colored streamers and flowers from paper. We hired a DJ who would play American music from *Grease* and *Saturday Night Fever*. We dressed in our best clothes and planned to dance until we could no longer stand. I wore my brown Levi corduroys, a floral blouse, and wooden platform shoes. We drank Cola Champagne and ate our chicken sandwiches as if we were aristocrats. The things we couldn't afford all year flowed freely for one night. We believed this was a good omen for our futures.

Only one hour passed before we heard gunshots. The music stopped. We all dropped to the floor and huddled in the darkness beneath the tables. The next thirty minutes consisted of silence, interrupted by sporadic bursts of gunshots that lingered in the air, hissing. Were our families safe in their homes? None of us had a car, there were no

17

streetlights, and our houses were at least three miles away.

Ten of us lived near each other and agreed to walk together. We made our way swiftly and silently, with a quickly made white flag that we hoped would signal peace. We stayed close to the buildings, walking in a line like mice. Our heads and shoulders hunched low. I lived the farthest away, and Andres made the long journey by my side.

When we reached my home, my mother stood in the door, a little light flickering above her head. Her embrace squeezed the air out of me, and I could feel her trembling. *"Gracias a Dios, que llegaste."* Andres disappeared into the dark street. I wouldn't be able to call him. Nobody in our *colonia* had a telephone. Trust was something I needed in large volumes those days, and something that was quickly slipping away.

From that night forward, things were never the same. It wasn't even worth hanging out with my friends or Andres, knowing the chances of encountering the military in the streets were unavoidable. We held our youth group meetings twice a week during the day at the church to avoid any suspicion of conspiracy from the soldiers. We couldn't say much, so we spoke in glances.

My friend René, a *promotor,* led our youth group, and I was his assistant. One afternoon, after leaving a meeting, I heard gunshots nearby just as I got home. I ran to my neighbors to find René in the arms of his grandmother, shot dead. He was my age, nineteen.

Army trucks rolled down the streets with twenty to thirty soldiers in each one. As their numbers increased, they began harassing everyone they came across, regardless of whether they were from El Salvador or not, including Americans.

One night, they ambushed the church run by the convent of American nuns, the Maryknoll Sisters. *Madre Magdalena,* the head nun, managed to ring the church bells when she heard their heavy footsteps on the roof, and when the church bells rang, the soldiers retreated.

My association with the Maryknoll Sisters was always risky. The government saw them as enemies, not just for their work educating marginalized communities about their rights, but because they supported the poor and stood against the government's abuses. In a time when any form of opposition was met with violence, their actions were seen as a threat. They were safe this evening, but it wouldn't last.

On December 2, 1980, three of the sisters were murdered and left in a ditch, shot dead as they tried to leave the country. The government had long targeted those who fought for justice, and this was just another tragic example of the lengths they would go to silence those who opposed them.

Chapter Five

Mamá, I Must Leave

We could feel the change in the weather. The leaves had begun falling from the trees. Late fall was a beautiful time in El Salvador, and it also marked the start of a couple of months when my 14-year-old brother, Oscar, and I were out of school and working in San Salvador at a clothing store that sold men's apparel. We enjoyed doing the job because it meant that at the end of December, we would return home with gifts for our mother and sister.

We prepared to return on a cold and windy New Year's Eve in 1979. We were so excited and couldn't wait for the last-minute shoppers to leave so we could close the store at 8:00 p.m. As more and more people showed up wanting to buy their last-minute pair of pants, we began to worry that we would miss the last bus to Santa Ana.

As we ran to the station, I knew it was late, and if the bus were there, we would probably have difficulty finding a seat. We made it in time and couldn't believe how many people were trying to get on board to spend New Year's Eve with their families back home. It was such a joyful time of celebration, with music and laughter filling the streets. People would gather outside at midnight to watch fireworks and celebrate together, and the air would become thick with cologne because everyone wanted to smell good for their end-of-the-year hugs.

When we finally reached the front of the line, we had no choice but to hop on top of the bus with the chickens, as every single seat was taken. I looked at the young face of my brother Oscar, who was so excited to go home, and said, "Hey, are you ready to go up to the top of the bus with all those chickens?" He looked at me and said, "Of course, let's go. We gotta get home, give momma and sister their gifts, and eat *panes con pollo.*" So up we climbed for the hour-and-a-half trip home.

The breeze felt so lovely and fresh, while the chicken's wings flapped in our faces, and our eyes watered as the bus driver drove way too fast, also wanting to get home to his family's celebration. I remember how happy my younger brother and I were. The chickens would start clucking and making noises, and we would laugh and say to them how lucky they were that they were safe tonight, because it was far too late to turn them into *panes con pollo* for the festivities. I never imagined this would be one of the last New Year's Eves I would celebrate with my brother. This would be the last fun adventure we'd share as teenagers.

When Oscar and I returned home that night, we noticed things were different. It was quieter, and the music was not as loud coming from each house. People celebrated inside their homes, and there were no social gatherings outside. It was all so very different.

You could feel the wave of sadness, desperation, and tremendous fear that weighed heavily on our community. My mother did her best to make things feel normal and festive. She had made a small chicken with delicious rice and a salad with the bit of money she had. You could tell she had put it together with so much love. She told us that we would be celebrating indoors. "You can put the music on quietly and dance, but as soon as we hug for the New Year, we're all going to bed."

At that moment, I could see that she was no longer the same happy person, trying to hide her fears. I saw in her beautiful black round eyes how much she wanted to protect us from the kidnappings and killings taking place at the hands of *Escuadrón De La Muerte*. She knew that things were changing and that she could no longer shelter us from these dangers.

Antonio had just returned from the United States to convince his girlfriend, Mirna, to return with him. Mirna was a member of our Catholic Church youth group. She was terrified by the increased military presence in our *colonia,* and like me, she was young and very involved with groups that promoted social justice. We were the targets of the military mission.

Mirna came to me one day and invited me to go with them, saying that her boyfriend knew the way north. He had made the crossing once, and she said he would arrange the trip for us. I sat and listened to everything she had to share, and then I began to cry. I knew it was time, but the thought of being separated from my mother, my siblings, and my culture was overwhelming. My mother thought it was too dangerous and told me it was a bad idea, refusing to consider the offer or opportunity.

We had relatives and friends who had migrated to the United States. My uncle's wife had brought back the first present I had ever received from there: a colorful beaded purse from California. We all knew that going to the United States was an option, but only out of complete desperation. It was expensive, and people didn't come back.

After several days of arguing, tears, and more arguing, my mother agreed to call my *Tío* Ernesto and *Tía* Pacita in California. I didn't want to leave, but I also didn't want to die. I didn't see any other path forward. I waited outside the public phone booth in Santa Ana while my mom made the call, the tension moving from her tight grip on the receiver to her face as she listened to what they had to share.

Once she hung up, she stood inside the phone booth, staring out and studying my face silently. I imagined they had just shared horror stories of people trying to cross, and that she was in a state of shock. In truth, they had told her what she didn't want to hear.

"If you think that her life could be in danger, don't stop her. Let her go." Crying, she came out of the phone booth, walked past me, and went home without a word.

I tried to make her feel better by promising that I would find a job in the United States and help her with my younger siblings. I would work as hard as possible and send them everything I made. We both knew it was time and that we had no other options. I now realize I was making this promise to distract myself from my deep fear of leaving. I knew enough to be scared, but not enough to hold me back.

We began our quick preparations, packing clothes, cookies, candies, juice, and fruit into my small backpack. My mother sewed a pocket into my underwear, inside which she wrote my name and my aunt and uncle's Los Angeles address on a piece of paper.

"Put your money in here too, Dora, so nobody steals it from you." I had hoped to change my underwear more often than that, but she meant that I should wear these during the actual crossing. I had saved enough money for meals and the bus ride north. I put Salvadoran bills, the equivalent of about ten U.S. dollars, into the small pocket and zipped it shut.

My mother was a devout Catholic and typically only trusted her saints, the Virgin Mary, and her God. However, the night before I left, we went to her friend's house to get a tarot card reading about my trip. She told me that this moment required extra protection.

We sat in a candlelit room as her friend blessed and bathed me with floral water, reciting the divinations from the cards. Then, we made our way to the church to light a candle as a final seal of protection and security. She handed me a small Bible and told me to read Psalm 91. I tucked it into my backpack without knowing what lay ahead of me.

I didn't have any type of identification, not even a Salvadoran passport. I had never thought of leaving my country. I didn't know what a smuggler was, only that it was someone's job to ensure we traveled safely to Los Angeles. We had lost contact with my father, so I couldn't call to ask him what to expect. All my trust was in Mirna's boyfriend, Antonio, whom she called Toño, a guy I had never met.

We took seven days on that first journey, one week. We crossed into Guatemala and Mexico without documents. We went to Mazatlán, took a ferry to Baja, and then took a bus up the peninsula to Tijuana. There, we hired a local smuggler, a tall, nasty-looking man in a big hat that kept his face in a dark, menacing shadow. He was supposed to help us climb the fence, bring the necessary tools, and show us the easiest possible route, but he was terrible at his job. He really wanted to get Vilma and me, the single women, alone. He offered to take us on the "easy" route. I was barely nineteen and a virgin.

The night of the crossing, he pushed me against a building as we fell behind the rest of the group. Fortunately, his big, ugly hat slipped forward and blocked his attempt to kiss me. I ran as fast as possible to catch up with Mirna and Toño and never left their side again. I realized that night that it wasn't just my country I would need to run from. I wasn't leaving danger behind.

I don't remember how I climbed the fence in Tijuana. Maybe they gave us a rope. It's interesting how our body conceals certain memories from us. I remember dropping down on the other side, meeting the earth like a cement block, and then tumbling down a hill. Before I could see straight, the lights came on. Pow! Glaring spotlights transformed the black night, and our dust-covered faces were in disbelief.

This was the first time I had encountered authorities outside of El Salvador. I had only seen men from other countries twice in my life: the tall, blue-eyed soccer players from Argentina who walked our streets like gods, and the Mormons.

"¡Quédate abajo! Stay down!" A man in uniform with a gun in his hand was yelling inches from my face in bad Spanish. *"¡Abajo!* Stay down! Open your legs! ¡Abierto!" His hands moved up my legs, touching the underwear my mother had told me to wear.

Through tears, I told them that I couldn't go back to El Salvador. I told them there was a war and I would be killed, but my pleas fell on deaf ears. Without any question, the Border Patrol agents arrested me and told me that I could have one call. I called my uncle in California, the only U.S. phone number I knew. I told him I had been arrested, and I didn't know where they were going to send me. He told me to be strong, that there would be another way. Within hours, I was on a commercial flight back home.

It was my first time on an airplane, which would have been thrilling if it weren't for my shoes full of mud, my shackled hands and feet, my prized brown Levi's caked in dirt, and the fact that I was being deported. When I leaned out into the aisle, I could see people at the front of the plane traveling with visas receiving hot coffee and snacks. The incredible difference in our experiences was overwhelming.

On the bus from the airport in San Salvador, I panicked as we got closer to my neighborhood. I would have to get off the bus in front of armed soldiers, and they would wonder why I had left. As if dead Salvadorans on the streets, young bodies left without care, and eyes closed as if they were simply sleeping, wasn't enough. I always worried they would wonder what I was hiding.

I managed to leave the bus unnoticed and snuck through the back streets, keeping my head down and my backpack clutched to my chest. I made it home without anyone noticing, and from that moment on, I hid in my house, avoiding everyone and everything. I was shut down with paranoia and fear, terrified of being tortured or executed in the middle of the night. My mother shared my worries.

On March 23, 1980, Archbishop Oscar Arnulfo Romero used his sermon to address the soldiers. He told them that God's law forbade them from continuing to kill their fellow citizens. The next day, he was killed while saying mass at the chapel *La Divina Providencia.* A gunman shot him at close range, right through the heart.

The country broke out in massive protests and bombings after he was murdered. The loss was catastrophic. The archbishop was the holy voice of the common people of El Salvador, the voice of those without a voice. The military fired rifles into the crowds at his funeral, killing dozens.

I called my aunt and uncle in Los Angeles. I was more scared than I had ever been. If he wasn't safe, I wasn't. They agreed, "We are scared for you, too. We'll help you to come up."

My mother did everything to ensure I crossed safely. Her adopted brother, *Tío* Carlos, and my seventeen-year-old cousin, Ricardo, would accompany me. We hired two smugglers in the capital city, paying each $2,500. This kind of money was unheard of within my community, and certainly not in my family. My aunt had found a way to borrow it from someone, and I knew it would take years to pay it back, if it were ever possible.

My mother spoke very little during this period of preparation. She didn't want to tell anyone I was leaving again, and she was worried about alarming the community or drawing attention to us.

"I hope you don't come back," she told me during those final days of preparation. I knew she said this for my protection, but my heart shattered into a million pieces when I heard those words. "Read your Bible, *hija*. Psalm 91. You are going to be okay."

And once again, I was off.

It was April, and 45 of us were crammed onto a bus headed to Yuma, Arizona. As I thought about what lay ahead, I was most afraid of jumping into the canal when we reached the border because I didn't know how to swim. All I could see was an image of myself drowning, and it was causing panic to set in.

The others on the bus around me were sharing stories of the military looking for them in their homes, of their family members disappearing, and of their friends being killed. As I listened, I felt my resolve return. If I drowned, so be it. I had to try. I understood that by staying home, I wasn't only endangering myself but also putting my family at risk.

Near the border, we walked for five hours through the Mexican desert, battling a whipping wind and navigating a long series of hills, followed by flat, soft earth. My feet sank into the sand like I was wading through muddy water. I fell often, each time covering myself in a cloud of dust that made it impossible to stop coughing.

When we finally came to a swampy area, we were told we were only a mile from the border, and on the other side, it would be only a few hundred feet to three cars that would safely transport us to our new homes. I now know this is the same lie shared with many on their journey north. They are assured that they are almost there and that plenty of help awaits them.

As we crested the hill, I could see the highway. When we exited the bus, I tried to look for the three cars parked along the road, but couldn't focus through the sea of moving lights.

I looked ahead at the canal, a concrete culvert with vertical sides and a five-foot span full of rushing water. If I fell, it would be impossible to get out. I watched as a few others crossed it successfully. They were all taller than I was, and I would need a running start, but they gave me the confidence I needed. I didn't look down, closed my eyes, and willed my legs to move. When I opened them again, my feet were on the other side.

The horizon of the United States sprawled out in front of me, and although the danger outweighed the excitement, I could see my future. I looked for the escape cars, scanning the dark desert floor for a path, but I saw a strange scene of chaos instead. Women, children, and men, all zigzagging down the hill, their eyes wild with terror.

I turned around to see multiple four-wheel-drive vans cutting up from the highway and coming straight at us. Within moments, the Border Patrol's headlights were shining on my face. I knew then that my second chance to start a new chapter in the U.S. would come to an end. We were rounded up and arrested, feeling as if this had been the goal of the smugglers all along. They had their money and were safely on the Mexico side of the border. They didn't care.

The bus we sat on must have been designed to look like a jail cell. It was entirely made of metal with no windows. Everyone was handcuffed and covered in dirt. They took us to San Ysidro, where our biographical data was recorded, and we were flown back to Mexico City that same night.

We were herded like cattle, moved from holding facilities to the edge of the airport runway, then to the end of a road, and onto a bus. The Mexican guards called us the ugliest words they could think of. They told us that Salvadorans were more trouble than anyone else as they shoved us toward the bus. It seemed as if our presence was a personal insult to them. We were the recipients of a targeted hatred I had never experienced before.

When I arrived back home, my mother was beside herself. She always had her rosary close to her, but that night, she brought it into the shower and slept with it. She blessed me with the Holy Cross every moment that she was in reach of my head.

"Look, you came back. It doesn't work." She was losing hope. And the pain of knowing what I went through was too much for her.

"But *Mamá,* the money we paid the smuggler came with a guarantee." He was supposed to get us across safely, which I could hardly imagine was possible at this point. The money we had given him allowed us two attempts. That in and of itself should have prepared us for the fact that this was in no way a one-time ordeal and that I would likely come back again and again.

"He said this time we're going to get on an airplane and fly to Los Angeles."

I did not trust him.

"This time, *Mamá,* I must leave. I promise I won't come back."

Chapter Six

My Third Attempt

I began my third attempt to cross into the United States with the same smuggler from my last trip, Jorge. It was at the height of summer heat in June 1980. I had found his business in the newspaper and had to read between the lines to determine what was actually being offered. It stated that his agency would provide vacation trips to the United States, with all border crossings arranged.

This trip included children with families and four unaccompanied minors. It was dangerous to be traveling in such a large group through Mexico. If the Mexican immigration officials stopped the bus for a surprise inspection, we could get a disastrous fine or even rough treatment and deportation back to El Salvador. But Jorge was greedy. He wanted to make a name for himself. He was confident about the trip despite failing at our earlier attempt. He told us that the details had all been arranged, that we were practically there, and there was nothing to worry about.

He had a leering nature, which was incredibly uncomfortable and irritated me from the start. He was dark and heavyset, half fat, half muscle, with shoulder-length black hair and a full mustache. I did not trust him, but I had no choice but to. He had a way of staring at women that was considered rude and unacceptable in El Salvador. He made nasty propositions. I feared antagonizing him and knew to stay out of his reach. I knew I had no choice but to go along, and my previous trip had made me a bit wiser and more cautious.

Three sisters were traveling with us, headed to Los Angeles to be reunited with their mother. At sixteen, Alicia was the oldest. She told Jorge she was eighteen so she could make the journey alone with her sisters. Alicia was slim, had pale skin, dark eyes, and short, curly black hair. The 12-year-old Juanita was also skinny and fair-skinned like her oldest sister. She had blonde hair, blue eyes, and naturally red lips. At 14, Inés was heavy and had a scar on her lower lip, which she hated. Inés told me more than once that her mom had promised her that when she got to America, she could finally have surgery to get it fixed.

Their mother had left for the "land of opportunity" when they were much younger. They had not seen her in many years. When she arrived in the United States, she didn't expect to clean homes for work. After sending money home to the girls, there was little left for her to survive on.

Disappointed, she had been unable to save enough to pay for her children's passage north. As the situation in El Salvador became dire, she decided to borrow money to pay the smuggler. He guaranteed a safe, well-supervised trip for the girls. The coyote promised they would be flown across the border and land near Los Angeles.

I loved spending time with these three girls. At nineteen, I felt like their older sister.

Being stuck on the bus for so long was hard, but we had much to discuss. We spent hours sharing our dreams about living in the United States. They teased me about my frequent and boisterous laugh. We were sometimes more excited about where we were going than saddened by what we had left behind.

Having my seventeen-year-old cousin Ricardo on this trip was helpful, and I especially enjoyed the company of my funny, irresistible Uncle Carlos. He gave most of the people on the bus nicknames, which lightened the mood.

He could usually be found sitting on an armrest, talking to someone, or sleeping in the aisle, as there weren't enough seats on the bus for all passengers. The three of us had decided to make another attempt together, and I was grateful for their presence.

Traveling with us were quiet students from church, a married couple, the Pagáns, who kept to themselves, and a plump middle-aged lady named Berta, affectionately called Rollers for always wearing hair curlers in preparation for being reunited with her husband.

José, in his early forties, had a beautiful singing voice and played a guitar that we had all chipped in to buy so he could entertain us.

There was an older, devout gentleman, Don Cruz, who always had his Bible open on his lap, and Guadalupe, an elderly aunt who cared for her frail niece, Felícita, who was in her early twenties.

There were middle-class individuals who had lost their income during the civil war and were forced to go north to support their families, as well as many others.

My uncle nicknamed me Yo-Yo because I was always making trips up and down the aisle to visit with people. Almost forty adults, seven or eight children, and infants were on the bus.

On this second attempt with Jorge, we took the same route on buses through El Salvador and crossed into Guatemala using fake passports and visas Jorge provided. We had to pay a 'tax' to the Guatemalan border guards, just like we had to pay *la mordida*, the bite, to Mexican officials. The tourist visas were only good until Mexico City, and we would travel far beyond that.

To get into Chiapas, Mexico, we were ferried across a river by local Guatemalans. They had made boats from inner tubes of truck tires with planks of wood placed across their girth for makeshift seats. I was strapped to one and pulled across the river by a man with a rope tied to his waist. He had to swim furiously as the water deepened and became faster.

Through all of these experiences, many of us on the journey became close. Shared trauma tends to bond people. We were getting to know one another, supporting each other, and forming a community.

We traveled for four days through Mexico, all crammed onto one bus without enough seats. Two chauffeurs took twelve-hour shifts driving, one all day and one all night. The off-duty driver slept on a shelf above the last row of seats. It was efficient, but it meant that for four days and nights, we had no breaks or opportunities to get away from one another. There was no privacy, no place to retreat and find some quiet or stillness.

Being with others was fine for some of the livelier folks, like my uncle and me, who constantly joked. However, for the introverts, it was difficult. The strain of being forced into contact with such a large number of strangers gave some people headaches and brought on anxiety. Those who wanted to be alone were seen as stuffy. It was taken as a rebuke. The contrasting personalities began to cause friction, and we all developed aches and fatigue from spending so many days confined to the bus. Not to mention, we had moved into July, and the temperature continued to rise.

There were no bathrooms, so we frequently stopped for food and restroom breaks, offering fleeting moments of relief. We made it through intense Mexico City and the long, tortuous route to Guadalajara.

When we arrived, we were happy to find *un puesto*, a food booth selling quesadillas. Excited to eat food from our homeland, we all ordered, only to find out they were so spicy that many of us couldn't finish them. Our native food is generally relatively mild, made without chiles. A reminder that although some things may look the same, we were far from the familiarities and comforts of home.

We traveled up the west coast of Mexico, and the landscape changed as we headed north. We saw sand, gravel, cactus, and dead-looking bushes everywhere. It seemed like a wasteland after the lushness of El Salvador. Mexico looked barren, inhospitable. The heat radiated from the hard earth and beat down from the broiling sun. We were sweltering in the bus but had to keep the windows closed to prevent dust clouds from rolling in. But even without the windows open to bring a slight relief, a fine silt filtered in, coating our skin, hair, clothing, and food.

We were in the midst of the great heat wave of 1980, during which temperatures averaged 110 degrees. Eventually, this heat would cause 1,265 deaths in the United States. At the time, there had been newspaper reports of over 100 deaths in the U.S. in the past ten days. Hundreds of thousands of chickens died within minutes of the fan in their henhouse failing. The pavement was getting so hot that it exploded. But we knew nothing about any of this. We knew we were suffering, crammed together on this stale and unbearable bus.

The view out the windows discouraged us, left us feeling flat. You could almost hear the questions swirling in everyone's head: *What have we done? Did I make the right choice? Where are we!?* I would no longer run up and down the aisles visiting with and encouraging others. José and his guitar remained silent.

We stopped on the outskirts of Hermosillo, Sonora, Mexico, as Jorge and the two other Salvadoran smugglers, Alvarado and Espinoza, attempted to devise a plan to bypass an inspection station. We were glad to no longer be on the bus, but we did not like being stuck in a cheap hotel waiting, ten women in one room. We weren't allowed out in case someone recognized our accents or one of the children gave us away.

We could only eat what Jorge or the other guides brought back from the market. None of us trusted Jorge. He liked to drink when he should have been sober. He wanted to play when he should have been serious. He was temperamental and did not keep his word. We were trapped in that hotel room for four days while we were sure he was passing the time at the bars.

The smuggler, Alvarado, was an experienced coyote. I hoped he could quickly gather the necessary information to continue our journey. On the fourth day, vans finally came for us before sunrise and drove us down a dirt road into the desert. They dropped us in the middle of nowhere, and we walked for four hours to bypass the inspection station to avoid the *federales* near Sonoyta. The bus driver awaited us on the other side.

When we finally arrived near the border, there was absolutely nothing there, not a single tree or bush. The only thing within sight was an abandoned one-room schoolhouse made of concrete blocks. We entered the building through its broken door and found a bare room with cracked floors and holes in the walls. However, the concrete blocks created shade, making it a much cooler place than the bus.

The bus driver told us he was leaving, so we hauled our luggage into this abandoned school and waited for what was next. We sat with our luggage all around us, cut off from any transportation or supplies, while our Salvadoran smugglers hitchhiked into town to contact the local Mexican guides who would lead us across.

I don't know how much time passed, but someone noticed a wiry barefoot boy coming slowly across the hard earth carrying a heavy bucket of water. He had hauled it from a small home some distance away. He told us that he knew there was no water in the school and that we could not survive without water. We hadn't realized how parched we were. Each of us drank deeply from the dipper, and the child made the trip again to help his sister with a second bucket.

We later discovered that we had drunk all his family's water reserves. They didn't have a well, and they paid to have it hauled in once a week. We quickly took up a collection to pay them for their water, apologizing repeatedly for leaving them without this precious resource.

Jorge returned with two hard-looking men driving two trucks. They belonged to a large gang known as *Los Muñecos*, The Dolls. They would drive us into the desert, but they were not the ones who would guide us across the border. They told us we needed to cross at a different place without explaining why or where that might be. It seemed as though we were constantly at the mercy of others, having to do exactly what they said without the privilege of any information. We climbed into the back of the trucks and bounced on the hard, wooden floorboards for two hours.

We arrived at a restaurant on the outskirts of Sonoyta and quickly realized that the group had been separated. The mothers and their babies were no longer with us. When we asked Jorge where they had gone, he said they had been sent with Alvarado to cross at Yuma, AZ. Alvarado was the only Salvadoran smuggler who had successfully crossed into the United States before, and I was upset to hear he would not be with us. What angered me more was that part of our group had disappeared without a chance to say goodbye. Jorge told us they would be taking an easier route because of the children. This only upset me further. I crossed my arms over my chest and glared at him, squeezing back tears of sadness, anger, and deep disappointment.

Jorge sent us into the restaurant a few at a time so we wouldn't draw attention to ourselves; there were 26 of us still together. We each had a filling meal of rice, beans, salad, and enchiladas. The food soothed our anxieties. We were at the threshold of our goal, so we celebrated with a bit of beer as José once again played his guitar.

There was always tension between Jorge and the other coyotes. The smuggler, Espinoza, provided a bit more assurance, but he was second in command. The complications on the trip never seemed to end. No one trusted that Jorge could or would do a good job. He often turned to me when people questioned him harshly. I made people feel good, and everyone talked to me. He didn't know how to handle the people he was responsible for or the situations that arose.

There were no rooms for us that night. The men slept on the ground, while many women slept in the back of the truck, and the others were inside an abandoned Datsun. Those of us in the truck bed were wedged together, sharing our warmth, looking up at the night sky, and wondering about our futures. It was a fleeting, beautiful moment, blanketed with an incredible closeness. I would carry that feeling to get me beyond the disaster yet to come.

We waited the next day for the guides to arrive. It had already been eight days since we had left El Salvador. The men hadn't stopped with the one celebratory beer we all had at dinner. They continued to drink and get loud, including my younger cousin Ricardo. I feared for him when more gang members came into the restaurant. The Dolls were a large gang that ran the border for hundreds of miles in each direction, and they were unpredictable and violent. They were waiting for another group of migrants to lead across. Always waiting for more people who were nothing more than dollar signs to them.

Two men arrived who we thought would be our guides,

but ultimately were not. They looked each of us up and down, assessing our ability to cross. They spent too much time with the women and asked a few if they wanted to cross easily in a car. Their meaning was clear. None of them took them up on their offer. They told us we would probably have to walk for a few hours through the desert and that they didn't think some of us had appropriate shoes, especially the women wearing high heels. We were dressed for the airport, where Jorge had told us we were going. One of the men left with a few women to buy tennis shoes in Sonoyta and returned half an hour later.

That evening, we learned that we were responsible for collecting and carrying our water. No one had told us this before, so we rummaged through a garbage heap alongside the restaurant and found gallon-sized milk jugs. We rinsed them and filled them at a faucet on the side of the building. It was primarily women doing this because many men were still drunk and paid no attention to the announcement.

Out of the thirty of us who would cross, which included the four guides, only eighteen carried water. The jugs were heavy. We wondered if it was worth it since we would only walk for a few hours. Jorge had told us it would be a half-hour walk. Someone else told us it would be ten miles, a bit more if there were trouble. What this trouble might be, we were never told, nor were we forewarned, so we could be prepared. But there was a sense that things were unraveling around us.

We all climbed into the back of the truck and headed out again. After fifteen minutes on the paved road, we veered off into the desert and traveled under the pale light of the quarter moon without lights. Don Cruz offered a prayer. Jorge ensured he had an address for each of us in the United States. Many of us still owed him more money.

Suddenly, a shrill whistle sounded from the dark. Jorge whistled back. A tall, thin man in his mid-twenties with straight hair and a cold, severe look on his face appeared with an older man in his early sixties. Though his face was worn, he looked much kinder than the younger one, and it became evident rather quickly that the pair's son was in charge.

He told us we had a strenuous walk ahead and wouldn't arrive at our pickup spot until after dawn, much longer than we had been told. He asked to see our water and was unhappy with what he saw, but there wasn't time to go for more.

I stood on the precipice of my new life. On one side was the fear of my government. On the other hand, the United States offered opportunities. But to get there, I would have to walk into the wilderness with two strangers I could barely see in the darkness. Would it be worth risking such helplessness? Did I really have any other choice at this point? I squeezed through the sharp strands of the barbed wire fence that two men pulled apart, held open for me, and stepped again onto U.S. soil.

Chapter Seven

The Desert Has No Mercy

We headed into the night with the nameless Mexican coyote in the lead. His father, Felipe, was at the rear, watching for stragglers and listening for sounds behind us. We immediately found that our shoes were inadequate for walking in the desert, especially at night. There were rocks of many sizes that we stepped on, maneuvered around, and tripped over. Some were gravel-sized, others the size of baseballs, grapefruits, and large boulders.

Guadalupe wore a pair of dress sandals with thin soles, and the hard, rocky ground had already begun to bruise the bottoms of her feet. Why hadn't the smugglers gotten better shoes for her? Also, her usual routine of housework had not prepared her for the rigors of hiking. Joining her at the rear of the line was the woman dubbed *La Gorda,* the Fat One, and older Don Cruz, still clutching his Bible.

No one was prepared to climb the Puerto Blanco Mountains. No one had sturdy hiking boots. No one had a map of the area, including, we would later discover, our guides. We were utterly dependent on the two Mexican smugglers to take care of us, and we were beginning to understand that this would not be a simple walk to freedom.

The short, shrill whistles of the father and son directed us. If one of us wandered off the trail and got lost, they would whistle, and we would follow the sound back to the group. We would whistle birdlike calls to indicate when we were back on track.

We were in the Organ Pipe Cactus National Monument, a nature preserve that helped us cross the United States undetected. This meant that we were surrounded by cacti everywhere. There were tall, many-armed saguaros that looked like giant, threatening people in the obscure night. Ocotillo reached out to snag us with its grey sticks branching up from a central bundle in spine-covered verticals higher than my head. Waist-high barrel cacti and their cousin, the fishhook cactus, made us zigzag right and left to get around them. Even the bushes and trees were covered with spines. The crucifix tree was perfectly named, with spikes three inches long running down every branch.

There was no path and absolutely no way to walk in a straight line. We were weaving around the sharp rocks and boulders, trying not to twist our ankles and trip. We got wounded by countless cactus spines. We had been trying to follow the younger guide's order to be quiet, but we kept getting stabbed and would shriek out in pain.

It was the cholla cactus that was the worst. Endless varieties! Short bunches growing no more than a foot tall looked innocent until we grazed them, and they embedded in our feet and ankles. Other types that grew to six feet had branches with loose bundles the size of tennis balls, densely covered by vicious spines. There were limitless jabs of pain, millions of them. Simply brushing against the plant embedded the needles into our flesh. The entire ball of spines would pull off the plant and attach to our clothing, then penetrate our skin, where it would deeply anchor itself.

I screamed the first time I brushed against a Cholla. My cousin was in no shape to help me because he was suffering from a hangover after drinking the day and night before. My uncle approached to help. With each pull of a needle, my skin lifted, and shreds of flesh were torn away. My arm was bleeding, and so were my uncle's hands. He finally resorted to pulling the spines out with his teeth while unsuccessfully keeping them from embedding in his tongue.

With our thin shoes and inability to see clearly at night, these thorns entered our feet and ankles. They covered our entire legs, arms, and faces. We had never encountered anything like a cactus in El Salvador or even seen a desert. Sometimes, we used two rocks to pinch the thorns and pull them out. Our line, which had started following closely behind the guide, began to lengthen, separate, and wander. We became like an accordion, stretching and contracting. We all suffered from more scratches and piercings from the plants we had to squeeze around or fall into while trying to avoid boulders. We were at the mercy of the desert.

We hadn't started with enough water to begin with, and the men who had been drinking for days guzzled most of what we had carried, their hangovers making them thirsty. They even poured some over their heads to cool off their bodies. It was still the first night. We were beginning to understand what we had gotten ourselves into, and still had no idea what we were in for. The three young sisters were tiring quickly. Don Cruz was struggling to walk because of his asthma and age. Guadalupe, in her tattered sandals, and *La Gorda*, under her excess weight, were limping and drained.

I heard someone ask the older guide, Felipe, how much farther we had to walk. He replied that he did not know and that we would have to ask his son. I pushed the thought out of my mind that only one person knew the way through these mountains, through this desert of heat and horrors, and that he was surly and angry. We didn't even know his name because if something went wrong, he didn't want us to be able to identify or locate him. He remained anonymous for his own safety.

We had to scramble on hands and knees to climb some of the mountains and slide precariously on the loose volcanic stone that covered the hills. Each time we made it over a mountain, the front guide would say, "The next mountain is our last." After a while, it became clear that he would say anything to keep us moving, like when he said there was a big lake up ahead where we could refill our water. The idea of a lake out there was ridiculous.

At one point, he banged two rocks together to get our attention. "I won't lie to you about this. I don't know this way. I don't even know where I am. I told my boss that I didn't know this route and that it would create problems. I told him I would get everyone lost. He told me not to worry, just do what he said."

The guide let loose a long string of swear words, then went on. "He only sent us this way because he was angry. One of you women wouldn't go with him across the border in a car. I think he wanted to teach you all a lesson."

I stood in silence, unable to find words to express my outrage at such senseless cruelty from the cartels who we had paid a lot of money and were directing and in control of our passage. Others shouted out, enraged. No one could believe the words that had just come from this young guide.

"Silence!" the coyote hissed at us. "There was an easier route I wanted to take, but it was forbidden by the boss. I don't know how much farther we have to walk."

And so, we walked, each of us withdrawing more into ourselves as we struggled against the pain and fatigue. I searched for strength. I called upon my faith. I was a devout Catholic and had just graduated from a Catholic high school. I truly believed there was a God and that God would save me from this. The strength of that belief kept me walking.

I also had a lot of physical strength from being a Cub Scout leader. We would walk several kilometers from Santa

Ana to the nearest lake. My body was more conditioned than others, yet we all suffered from the unrelenting heat, being repeatedly pierced and scratched, and our lack of water.

The dark we started our walk in had been difficult, but the dawn now brought problems. We could see each other rather than the vague shapes stumbling along together. Now I could see Felícita vomit and rub her hand across her head where I knew it throbbed. I could see the graphic records of the cactus wounds, the scratches, the blood. The dawn also brought the heat. Where it had been in the high eighties during the night, the early July daytime temperature would rise to 110, 115, 120 degrees. The ground would become even hotter, up to twenty or thirty degrees more than the air temperature.

It never cooled off, especially in areas where the soil was dark and held the heat. It was hard to believe we had already left June behind and were moving into one of the hottest months of the year. We were out of the mountains now and entering the desert, descending into the Valley of the Ajo. Still, we kept going, carried forward by the hope that somewhere ahead of us was our way out.

The coyote yelled, *"Migra!* Hide! Everybody, get behind something, quick!"

I could hear the thumping beat of a Border Patrol helicopter approaching, but there was no place to hide. All around us were rocks, cactus, and flimsy thorn-riddled bushes. I found a slight depression and scooped dirt over my clothes. Don Cruz had fainted and lay exposed. There was nothing we could do about that. He was too heavy to drag, and there was virtually nothing to hide under. But they passed overhead without seeing us.

We had been walking since nine the night before, and it was now eight in the morning. Eleven hours straight. It felt good to lie down for a while, especially after my heart quit racing and I knew we were safe for the moment.

The Sonoran Desert is one of the driest places on the continent. The morning air temperature rose to over 110 degrees. The breeze felt like a fire blowing at my face, and the day was just beginning.

"Let's go back." I heard someone say. Of course, the two Salvadoran smugglers – Jorge and Espinoza – who were making a fortune off us, $65,000 from the 26 in our group (roughly $250,000 today), kept insisting, "No, no. We can't go back. You guys are going to be okay."

They had no mercy. They had no mercy. They just kept repeating, "Keep going, keep going," even though, like us, they had no idea where we were or how far we had to go.

The arguments about water intensified. Some people were willing to share the small amount they had. Others would not. When I rose, I was wobbly and weak. My uncle loosened his belt so I could hold onto it, and he pulled me along. He had stolen a long drink of someone's water and had the strength to help others. Plus, I am sure he felt guilty about drinking so much of our water supply to try to alleviate his hangover.

By mid-morning, all our water was gone. During our next break, my uncle attacked a saguaro after hearing it contained water. It was the first time we had taken action to help ourselves. Until then, we had always followed the coyotes, trusting they would care for us, only to realize that everything they had told us was a lie.

Why did everyone lie? Did they not think we couldn't handle the truth? Did they not realize that the truth might actually help us get through this nightmare?

We had risked everything to escape the danger back home. We would never have put ourselves at the mercy of such strangers otherwise. We were naïve about smugglers and the methods they used to cross. Once in the desert, the coyotes could do whatever they wanted with us. We were genuinely helpless.

Tio Carlos used a club he had made from the rib of a cactus to attack the saguaro. He finally knocked off an arm, and others joined him in his attempt to hack it open. The cactus flesh was bitter and terribly unpleasant, and it did nothing to moisten our lips or quench our thirst.

The father and son smugglers hadn't brought any water with them either, and they were becoming noticeably weaker. As I looked around, an uneasy sense of doom began to settle in. The son must have sensed it, too, because he switched from saying, "Hurry up, we have to get out of here," to "Don't panic. It's no use to panic. Let's go a little farther, and then we'll rest again."

At this point, our group split into the 'stop' or 'go' factions. Everyone belonged to one or the other. Some wanted to stop to relieve their agony from walking in the heat without water. Some wanted to continue at any price to end the horror and pain of wandering in the desert. All day long, this argument came and went. We were never able to resolve it because we were spread out widely throughout the desert.

The son, our lead Mexican coyote, wanted to stop. He told us we had missed our ride but that they would show up again tomorrow. Someone suggested we keep moving, but he wanted to stay and rest until nightfall, when the temperatures would decrease somewhat. Our confidence in him fell as our troubles increased.

As we moved farther into the desert, he seemed to be regaining his sense of direction as the mountains off in the distance came into sight. He believed these mountains had always served to give him his bearings.

I was exhausted, even with the help I had been receiving from my uncle. I took a step and everything went grey, then black. The next thing I felt was someone patting my cheeks. But as I came to, I realized that they weren't pats. They were slaps. My uncle was slapping me, trying to wake me up. He had me sip some Coca-Cola that someone had pulled out of their suitcase. The sweetness and moisture revived me.

"Let me look at your face," my uncle said.

He examined me carefully by running his fingers lightly over my skin. "You fainted and fell directly into a bush. I was afraid you had blinded yourself on the short, sharp branches." He dabbed at the blood on my cheeks, but I could see just fine. I sat crying and squinting into the blinding sun.

Don Cruz came up to us and handed me his jug. "Here, drink this. It's concentrated water." It was yellowish, and I thought it was orange juice, so I took a long swallow and quickly realized it wasn't water or juice. It was his urine… I gagged and vomited.

"No, no, Dora," Don Cruz said. "It's good for you. You need the fluid."

I couldn't drink it at that moment, but it made us all realize that it would be urine or nothing until we were out of the desert. Those of us who had kept our empty water jugs started to use them. We also pulled out our toothpaste and used it to moisten our mouths.

After lying down for a while, I recovered some of my energy. Some of the group continued, and I could see them about a quarter mile in front of us in a low area that almost completely hid them from view.

My cousin became unconscious, and once we had revived him, we found that he couldn't stand. José was also struggling. He had been hiking in his cowboy boots, and when we pulled them off, his socks were wet with blood. The rest of us were so weak that we could not stand, so we ended up crawling the entire distance to the other group, tearing the flesh on our hands and knees along the way. We joined them in the wash, a dry creek bed with steep sides. Three of the younger men there decided to walk toward the east, hoping to come to a road. They told us they would find water and bring it back.

In the wash, our young Mexican guide looked nervous as we moaned, twisting on the ground in pain. He walked up the side of the gully to look around, then came back down. "I told you not to walk during the day when it's too hot," he said. "You're a bunch of idiots. You won't make it unless you get some water. I know where to get some. I'll be back in about two hours."

He told us to keep moving, even after scolding us for not stopping in the heat. He said the farther we went, the easier it would be later. One woman had enough strength to follow him, while the rest of us did not. His father had not been seen for hours. We didn't realize it yet, but our Mexican guides had just abandoned us, and our Salvadoran smugglers were in the same horrible shape as we were.

We lay in the wash, trying to find shade under the few trees and bushes. In the desert, many plants shed their tiny leaves in the summer as a means of protection from the heat. We waited for the young guide to return, unsure whether he had gotten lost or injured, and had no idea whether he would return to us. We were burned. Our lips were swollen, split, and bleeding.

We realized that our urine was the most critical resource we had and started drinking it without concern to try to save ourselves. We all sacrificed our modesty and began to fill the empty water jugs in front of each other. We didn't have the strength to walk off to do it privately.

One of the young men found a bottle of Old Spice aftershave in his suitcase and swallowed half of it before he felt the pain of the alcohol hitting his dry, raw throat. He fell to the ground, screaming. I crawled over to him, crying for others to help, but nobody was able to move. I watched him arch in pain and then become unconscious. I had been holding onto the hope of drinking my tiny bottle of *Majada* perfume as a last resort, but now I knew that was not an option. I let my body fall flat on the ground and began crying for my mother.

Bertha, the young, overweight woman whom we had nicknamed *La Gorda*, had been lying silently on the ground, her body swollen and red. She cried for water, but none of us had any. She sputtered, making horrible sounds, and screamed about the pain in her chest.

"It hurts so much!"

She had a seizure. No one was with her when she died because she was traveling alone, and we were all too debilitated to help.

I was feeling sick to my stomach from heat exhaustion, but the terror of her death gave me strength. I got up and crawled to her. I gathered clothing from the ground and carefully covered her. I invited everyone else to come around her to say a prayer. I do not think any of us had thought we would die on this crossing. Maybe we would get caught and be returned, like what had happened to me before, but not die. We were all sobered and returned to our spots to rest until we could try to walk again.

My uncle who was always clowning around and could make everyone laugh said, "No shit she's dead, but I'm alive. I'm going to keep walking." He jumped up, thinking he could run, but he just fell forward.

We had walked about twenty miles from the border as the crow flies, but there were no straight lines in the desert. It felt like we were walking in circles, making no progress. How many miles had we walked in our ridiculously inappropriate shoes, tugging our suitcases behind us? How many hours? How many days? It was a living nightmare.

Carlos suggested that we start a fire so that someone might see us and we could be rescued. We argued over that, too. Ileana brought up that recently, there had been rumors of two plane loads of returning refugees being unloaded in a remote area of the airport in El Salvador, lined up, and shot by government troops. The bodies had been dumped in ditches along the same highway where the corpses of the three Maryknoll nuns had also been found on December 2, 1980.

"The guide could still come back with water," Pagán argued. "I don't want to bring *la migra* to capture us if we don't have to."

"It's a day of festivities in the U.S., Independence Day. There shouldn't be too many Border Patrol agents around," someone else argued.

"You're living in a dream world," my uncle said. He was impulsive, never taking much seriously, but in that moment, he was as terrified as the rest of us. We started a fire at the base of a power pole and began throwing on branches and dried plants, hoping to create a huge bonfire. The fire gave courage to one of the women in our group. She said, "I'm leaving. I don't want to stay here and wait for *la migra*. Who wants to go with me?"

Several said yes, but they didn't have the energy to walk. Finally, a man stood up, and they headed off into the night.

La Gorda's body began to decay in the heat. She was bloated and began to smell. We were going to have to leave her behind. We were not going to be able to keep animals from her. It was all horrible.

The fire was dying out, as the pole never ignited. We took burning sticks from the last of the fire and held them high over our heads so we could see in the opaque night. We limped slowly along, moving several hundred yards up the wash. Those of us who could still walk helped those who were struggling.

The night remained hot. We took turns drifting in and out of consciousness. As the night shifted from impenetrable black to deep blue, the Salvadoran smuggler, Espinoza, sat up. "We can't just give our lives away. We have to try something."

My uncle said, "Let's make an agreement that whoever dies first, even me, we'll open him up and drink his blood."

"What? You crazy fool!" others cried.

Espinoza said, "Let's walk some more. Maybe we'll find water so we can survive. Perhaps we'll find help."

One by one, the other men rose to go with him. There were eight of them, including my uncle and cousin. That left eleven women, plus old Don Cruz and Jorge. I wanted to go with the men, but they said no, they would be moving too fast and would have a better chance of finding water and getting back quickly without me.

When they asked Jorge to come, he said, "No. You're only going to get lost. I'm going back to Mexico and then home to El Salvador. I'm done with this mess." I thought the real reason he was staying behind was that he couldn't walk anymore and was too proud to admit it. When he added, "Plus, I'll protect the women," a shiver ran up my spine.

At the last moment, Don Cruz decided to join the men. "It's my duty to help," he said. I could see that the other men did not want him along. They were glancing at each other, shaking their heads. Even though they would not be walking fast, they knew that he would slow them down. But he was determined.

Someone came down into the arroyo and helped him up the embankment from the wash, but once on top, they turned their backs on him and headed off. Just like all of the others, they left us. I imagined Don Cruz being left soon, too, to die alone in the desert.

Ileana suggested we pray, so we knelt in a circle and tried

to pray, though we were struggling. Our bodies ached, stiff from the relentless heat and exhaustion, and the pain from our injuries made it hard to focus. Sweat dripped down our faces, mixing with tears we couldn't wipe away. We had no strength left, and each word we forced out felt heavier than the last. Still, we knelt together, desperate for any comfort, even if it was just the act of praying.

Most of us were naked except for our panties, trying to escape the heat. There was Guadalupe with her very ill niece, Felícita; Ileana with her pregnant sister-in-law, Luisa; the three young sisters; Pagán's wife; the woman from Chalatenango; Rollers; and me. As I glanced around the circle, I saw bodies marked by scratches, bruises, sunburns, torn skin, and cactus thorns embedded in our flesh.

Ileana led us in a confession. We all searched through our pasts to see if we could find any cause for our punishment. We took turns admitting whatever we could think of: meanness, falseness, things that shamed us. All I could think was that when I was seventeen, I drank a beer with friends who had gathered to talk about an upcoming service project. We repented, we asked for forgiveness. I did not feel better afterward.

When the men left, they took all the water jugs, so we passed around a plastic cup that we each squatted over. We shared what little fluid we had left in our bodies and used a stainless steel spoon to provide tiny sips for each other. When the cup got full, we urinated on rags that we held between our legs, then used on our faces to try and cool off. The woman from Chalatenango donated her tube of toothpaste, which we passed around, and each ate a little.

Felícita was weaker than the others because she couldn't bring herself to drink the urine. At one point, her aunt begged Rollers and Luisa to hold her hands so she could force her to drink. She spat it out, saying, "I don't want that. I just want to die now."

Her aunt told the others to let her go and gently wiped her niece's face, then held her in her arms, quiet and resigned. A short while later, I watched the frail young woman in her pink dress, a year older than me, die in the arms of her aunt.

Hours passed. Everything became more confused as waves of unconsciousness continually swept over us all. We were living in a nightmare that I would wake up in and fall asleep to for what felt like endless days and nights. I could hear coyotes yipping, but I didn't know what they were because I had never heard them before. Was it the devil coming to get us? I whispered, *"Ay, la llorona* is coming for us." We didn't know about snakes, either. Thankfully, no one suffered a snake bite, a venomous spider bite, or a scorpion sting, at least not that we knew about.

The woman from Chalatenango had put smooth stones in her mouth to try to force saliva. I heard gagging and looked up. She had turned a ghastly dark color and was ramming her hand into her mouth. She had swallowed a stone and was choking. I stumbled over as best as I could to help, but my fingers were too short. Jorge came over and pushed her over. He pounded furiously on her back, but he was only knocking the item farther down her throat. She started to spasm.

"The spoon!" Jorge cried. "Give it to me!"

I was relieved that someone knew what to do. Juanita grabbed it and handed it to him with a trembling hand. Chalatenango had gone rigid, and with all of Jorge's strength, he forced her jaw open. He dug the spoon in, trying to jam it behind the rock. Blood spurted out of her mouth. I grimaced to hear the spoon scraping on the rock.

Minutes passed. Jorge withdrew the spoon, wiping it on a rag. Chalatenango was limp and still. Juanita was crying, and her sister was trying to comfort her. I kept my head down and noticed my Bible lying on the ground. It had blood on it, and when I opened it, it fell to Psalm 91, the exact one my mother had told me to read before I left El Salvador. It was a prayer for travelers, and I read it out loud in my weak, scratchy voice.

Whoever dwells in the shelter of the Most High will rest in the shadow of the Almighty.

I will say of the Lord, "He is my refuge and my fortress, my God, in whom I trust."

Surely He will save you from the fowler's snare and from the deadly pestilence.

He will cover you with His feathers, and under His wings you will find refuge.

His faithfulness will be your shield and rampart.

You will not fear the terror of night, nor the arrow that flies by day, nor the pestilence that stalks in the darkness, nor the plague that destroys at midday.

A thousand may fall at your side, ten thousand at your right hand, but it will not come near you.

You will only observe with your eyes and see the punishment of the wicked.

If you say, "The Lord is my refuge," and make the Most High your dwelling, no harm will overtake you, no disaster will come near your tent.

For He will command His angels concerning you to guard you in all your ways; they will lift you up in their hands, so that you will not strike your foot against a stone.

You will tread on the lion and the cobra; you will trample the great lion and the serpent.

Because He loves me, says the Lord, "I will rescue him; I will protect him, for he acknowledges my name.

He will call on me, and I will answer him; I will be with him in trouble,

I will deliver him and honor him. With long life, I will satisfy him and show him my salvation."

I tried to find solace and protection in those words,

clinging to God's name.

Guadalupe seemed to gain strength from the passage because she got up and climbed out of the wash, hoping to see if anyone was coming back for us. She returned and said all she could see was the endless desert, shimmering with heat, barren and pale, stretching all the way to the mountains.

The middle sister, Inés, helped Luisa go through her bag, and they found her makeup kit. We decided to apply a base to our faces to protect our skin from further sun exposure. We painted each other's cracked, puffy lips with bright red lipstick. Then, Luisa started making raspy noises. She was pregnant, and the ordeal was especially difficult for her. "I'd like to die," she moaned.

Her sister-in-law crawled over to her. "No, you can't. You have a child to think of."

"I don't care. I feel too hot. I'm too thirsty. I miss my mother and father."

They were both crying now, one wanting to be done, the other wanting her to try to live. I heard Luisa ask for Ileana's pardon, and I mouthed Psalm 91 again, calling on the Lord to help.

"Jorge, kill me," Luisa pleaded. "I can't do this anymore. Kill me."

He crawled toward her, creeping closer. "Can I kill you?"

I watched her nod yes, though I could see terror in her eyes. He suddenly threw his heavy, fat thigh over her face. Ileana was still nearby, and she jumped on his back and began hitting him. I was too immobilized to help. She pulled his leg off, which enraged him. He kicked her repeatedly in the face and chest with his shoe. When she rolled over, he continued to kick her in the back. Once she was silent, he put his leg back over Luisa's mouth and held it there until her struggling ceased and she lay still.

I watched it all from nearby, huddled under my palo verde tree, trying to be invisible. When he turned my way, I scooted backward even further, but he wasn't interested in me. He moved toward the three sisters. Like us, he was delirious from thirst, hunger, and heat, but unlike us, he could still stand.

"She was the lucky one," he said. "She won't have any more troubles." He looked from one of the sisters to the next, assessing them. "I want to have sex with all of you before I die. I want to do everything before it's too late. Having sex is good. It makes you sweat, and sweat cools the skin. I'll let you lick the sweat off my body."

He turned to Pagán's wife and ordered her to hold Alicia. Pagán's wife had been directed by her husband for her entire adult life. She was so completely under his control that we never even learned her name. She was always just Pagán's wife.

Now, she was unbalanced from his absence and was delirious with dehydration and heat. When Jorge told us we were all going to die, she became insane. She grabbed Alicia's wrists and held them tightly above her head. Alicia was weak now and unable to free herself from the crazed woman's grip.

The youngest sister, Juanita, picked up the stick that Jorge had used on Ileana and began hitting Pagán's wife. She tried to duck the blows but would not let go of Alicia's wrists. I watched as Juanita hit her over and over in the face, on her shoulders, on her chest. Finally, she collapsed, covered in blood, almost unrecognizable from the beating. Juanita collapsed beside her in exhaustion.

Guadalupe and Rollers staggered away, knowing they were next in line. He hollered after them, "Don't go. I want you, too."

After going unconscious again, I woke up, and my body felt strange, like ants were crawling all over it, even though I couldn't see any. I heard grunting and looked across the wash and saw Jorge on top of Juanita, moving his hips and making noise. He held the spoon over her neck, pressing it deeply into the smooth hollow in the center of her collarbone. Her sisters lay motionless around her.

Oh my God. He killed them all, I thought. I knew he had a sick mind from our first trip. He was after every woman, constantly harassing us. We were just girls. I was still a virgin, and he knew that. In my gut, I knew he could sense that. During those times in El Salvador, we were pretty modest. He was always hunting and searching for something, someone.

I was frightened of him and pretended to be dead. I prayed he wouldn't rape and kill me, too. We were all desperate with dehydration and exposure, but who would do such things to dying people? It was total depravity.

Ileana regained consciousness, and Jorge saw her raise her head. He started moving toward her. She was too weak to stand, so she began rolling over rocks, sticks, and cactus to try to escape.

He finally reached her and hit her with a stick, then with his fists in her face, in her breasts, and in the stomach with all his might. Even after she was again unconscious and an unrecognizable mess, he continued to beat her.

Eventually, he staggered off, then fell. He got onto all fours, kicking and clawing at the ground, straining and turning purple. His body shuddered into silence. Stillness descended onto the desert once more.

I remember hearing voices, or maybe it was the wind, and thinking it was my mother calling me home. For a moment, I let myself drift toward that voice, toward rest, toward surrender.

Chapter Eight

The Rescue

I spent the night under a small tree, unconscious most of the time. I could no longer feel my legs. My lips were cracked and swollen. My vision blurred as I looked up at the night sky. I remember thinking, this is how it ends—out here, in the desert, without my family, without a goodbye.

When awake, I would mumble, "The Lord is my refuge, the Lord is my refuge, the Lord is my refuge." This was all that I could remember of Psalm 91. This is what hell feels like, I thought. I am already in hell. It was horrible. Each minute, I felt like I was dying and alone. I was waiting to die at this point.

At times, I thought everything around me was water under the most beautiful blue sky filled with millions of stars. It was the bluest blue I had ever seen. This vision guided me into a deep sleep.

"Don't die on me! Don't die on me!" A man was yelling right in my face.

"Water. Water. Water," I croaked.

"No, you can only wet your lips." The man rubbed water across my lips. "If I give you water, it will kill you."

People were everywhere, surrounding me from all sides. It had gone from complete silence to a loud, overwhelming noise. There were Border Patrol agents, motorbikes, and 4x4 trucks. National Park rangers were on horseback. A search and rescue team from the Pima County Sheriff's Office was deployed.

There were two Border Patrol Cessnas circling overhead, and the Customs Patrol helicopter was raising dust, making an incredible racket. An Air-Vac helicopter with a team of paramedics landed to help evacuate us. Press helicopters carrying extra water and equipment arrived from Phoenix. The noise was deafening, and it was all mixed with the smell of decomposing bodies.

"Oh, no, come back! You've got to live!" A uniformed man was yelling in my face again. He picked me up and carried my limp and almost lifeless body to a nurse who put an IV in my arm. I lay on a gurney, incredibly close to death. I was close enough to hear Ileana crying about her babies. She was still alive, which made me happy, even in my semi-conscious state. The rescuers began to worry that there were infants with us, but she was referring to her children, whom she had left behind in El Salvador.

I woke up in a hospital bed in Ajo, Arizona, about twenty miles from where we had been found. Everything was hazy. Nurses hovered around me, and some of them were crying. I remember thinking, *Am I in trouble? What happened?* My body ached all over, and my throat felt like sandpaper. I was so weak I could barely lift my head.

I stayed in the hospital for seven long days, with nurses constantly coming and going. They drew blood, took my temperature and blood pressure, and painstakingly pulled cactus spines from every inch of my body with tweezers and pliers—each prick a sharp reminder of the desert's cruelty. One nurse even cut my hair because the sun had burned it badly, leaving it dry and fragile.

A priest came and asked me to say the Lord's Prayer with him, but I was too weak to concentrate, and my throat hurt too much to speak. He said he would help me contact my mother, but it was days before I could write a letter. He sent it to a neighbor who delivered it to my mother, which was the only safe way to communicate during the civil war. I learned that my mother had thought I was dead for two weeks before that letter arrived. She had read my name in a list in the newspaper of those who had tragically died in the desert crossing in the United States.

I asked the priest about my uncle and cousin, who had left with the men's group, but he had no information. Fortunately, I did not have to suffer the grief of loss as my mother did, as I was soon told that they had both survived.

José came to visit me. When he walked into the room, he gave me a big hug. "Thank you," he said. "You helped save my life." That moment has never left me. His words were a gift I still carry.

I learned that the Border Patrol had found José and the men who had left the group to try to find help first. Later, I learned they had not moved far from us. It was all so sad because we were only a mile away from the road, from milepost 67 on Highway 85. But we were lost, dehydrated, suffering from heat exhaustion, and did not know which way to go. We had been out there for days without food or water in pounding, relentless heat. We had defied all odds by staying alive.

Some of the surviving men looked like they were wearing masks when they were found because they had spread toothpaste on their faces to protect their skin from the harsh sun. We thought the same when we put on makeup, that it might help protect our already blistered and cracked skin.

We must have looked frightening to the rescuers. Most of the men were naked or only wearing grimy underwear. In our delirium, we had all removed our clothes, thinking it would keep us cooler. Our abandoned belongings were scattered around the scene.

Some men had even shoveled dirt into their mouths,

convinced they had finally found water. I learned that my uncle was discovered with his head stuffed into an animal burrow under the roots of a small bush. He said it felt cool on his head while his body screamed as if it were being cremated. He pulled his head out when he heard the Border Patrol and said, "You have to find the women. Find the women! That way." He pointed west but didn't know precisely where we were. My cousin survived, too. Of the thirteen dead, eight were women. Twenty-six of us had crossed the border into the desert together, and half did not make it out.

They found us near Alamo Wash, a dry creek bed that would have eventually led us to the highway, but we were unable to walk and had no idea where we were or which direction to go. The town of Ajo had a Salvadoran exchange student attend its high school the previous year. They had supported him when three of his friends at home were killed by the death squads. Perhaps because of this, they understood more than most Americans why our group had attempted to cross the desert, seeking to escape our country. The townsfolk turned out to be very supportive and helpful.

They announced on the radio that we needed clothing, and enormous quantities arrived. They offered food, money, and jobs. One group began organizing legal aid assistance for us. A group of concerned Ajo citizens sent a telegram to their senators and representatives, writing, "We demand that the Salvadoran survivors be given protection from the violence of their home country. Aliens from other countries have received asylum, so should Salvadorans. People in Ajo are willing to house them."

The Salvadoran government was not happy with the publicity we were receiving. Reporters from around the world came to share our story, including those from Sweden, Italy, Australia, South Africa, England, Germany, and most of Latin America, as well as from all over the United States.

The Salvadoran Consul General came and treated me like I was an enemy of my country. The publicity we were receiving for leaving the country and many of us dying was a national embarrassment to our government. He never even asked why I had attempted such a journey three times. Later, he reported that we came here to make money, not because of the political situation in El Salvador.

People kept coming and going from my hospital room—nurses, doctors, even homicide detectives. I was too weak to speak most of the time, barely able to keep my eyes open. The nurses told me I had been just minutes from death when they found me. My body was shutting down, and it would take time to recover.

Once I was stable enough to leave, I was transferred to jail along with Guadalupe. It was jarring, going from a hospital bed to a cold cell. Meanwhile, Ileana had to remain in the hospital for several more weeks. She had been brutally beaten by Jorge, and her injuries were severe. The two men and the single woman who had left the group to go for help had made it to the road by the middle of the night. They had heard a car and headed in that direction. Finally, another vehicle passed on the road but would not stop for them. It swerved and then stopped. The driver set a gallon of water in the middle of the road and then drove on.

Eventually, these three were picked up by the Border Patrol, but when questioned, they all denied having traveled with others. They knew how badly we wanted to avoid being sent back, and they believed we might still be able to make it out. When they left us in the desert, no one had yet died. They had no way of knowing that the idea of moving on no longer existed for the rest of us. They could not know that at that point, we all rose and fell into different cycles of consciousness, moving from misery into delirium and oblivion.

The woman and man who had left our group earlier also made it out to the highway and were picked up by Border Patrol. They were interrogated for many hours, but they did not want to tell them that there were others. The woman could not stand the thought of all she had endured being for nothing. She had also never seen American immigration officials before and was intimidated and frightened.

At the end of another scorching day, she finally admitted there were others in the desert. Perhaps more of us would have lived if these people had spoken up sooner. I know they were doing what they thought was best for us, and I honestly don't know what I would have done in their situation. They didn't know we were out there dying.

It is a very tragic story. Our smugglers left us behind. These stories persist to this day, with the same lies being told, and the desperate still believing them.

When we were in jail, we received a special delivery letter in Spanish explaining that if we were poor, we could have a lawyer represent us without a fee. We all agreed to this and met with our lawyers in jail. In the trial, we would be held as material witnesses against the one Salvadoran smuggler who survived, Espinoza.

The older Mexican smuggler, Felipe, was in the same shape as we were, but recovered to face the trial. The younger Mexican smuggler, who had told us he was going to get water, had abandoned us and escaped back to Mexico. He not only left us but also his father to die in the desert. He was never found guilty.

This was not going to be a U.S. murder trial for the deaths of thirteen people, or negligence or abandonment. Instead, the case focused on the smuggling of undocumented immigrants into the United States.

I wouldn't come to understand the full scope of what

happened right away. Over the years, details trickled in. I later learned that a photographer had been sent out from the *Arizona Daily Star* newspaper when they heard on the police radio that a group of migrants were lost in the desert near Ajo. He was allowed to ride along with a Border Patrol agent.

I cannot imagine what he must have been thinking when he saw the dead bodies, some exploded in the heat, some gnawed on by animals, spread across the desert floor. Of the eleven women and one man at that site where I was found, only three of us were alive, and barely so. Some were so beaten that they were almost unrecognizable.

What a horror for him. The photo he took of my completely limp body being carried out by the Border Patrol agent who had pleaded with me not to die made the cover of *The New York Times,* a tiny 19-year-old girl in her panties and white shirt with tiny flowers. I was so close to death. That photo, along with others he shot at the scene, was also published internationally in *Paris Match, Stern* (Germany), *Life, Look, Time,* and *Newsweek* magazines.

We spoke by phone many years later. He said he never forgot what he saw.

"Oh my God, Dora, I've been wondering how you are all these years."

"Well, here I am. Do you want to know what I'm doing now?"

"I have heard something about your work. Send me a picture of you. I want to see what you look like."

We exchanged photos of our families and talked about our lives.

"I'm so thankful that you're alive and for what you are doing," he said.

I told him about the second time I was on the front cover

of *The New York Times*. He laughed, commenting on the rarity of this happening.

"Your photo started my relationship with newspapers," I joked. "They have been vital over the past forty years in helping get information out to the public about what is really happening at the border."

"We're lucky we live in this country where we still have freedom of the press," he said, before adding, "Mostly."

Chapter Nine

Finding Sanctuary
Tucson, Arizona, 1980

Germany, Canada, and Spain asked to have us sent to their countries, not to deport us back to El Salvador. They knew we would be killed because of the worldwide publicity of the trial. It was one of the first massive deaths in the desert of those fleeing the civil war in El Salvador, one that the United States was deeply in the middle of.

One day, an officer in the jail came and told me I was being released because a group of churches had helped pay for my bond. A Hispanic radio station found a family to sponsor me while the investigation was ongoing, and I was free to leave. That was the day when I began to feel safe, but my nightmares would not let me sleep for quite some time to follow. I was sad for all the people who had died in the desert, I was lonely for my family I left behind, and I was anxious about living with people I had never met.

Afterward, I learned that it was Manuel Artiaga on Radio Fiesta in Tucson who asked in Spanish if anyone could sponsor the migrants who had just survived the tragedy in the desert. Hearing his voice still makes me smile with thanks.

It was Reverend John Fife, a church pastor in Tucson, and his group who asked their network of churches for money. We each needed $750 to secure our bail and be released from jail. Our lawyers negotiated this to $500 each, but none of us had that kind of money. Only the smugglers had any money.

They had all our money. Reverend Fife coordinated with the other churches to pay our bail and secure our release.

This tragedy would mark a turning point in the United States. It would expose how the U.S. was denying asylum to Salvadorans and Guatemalans—people who were fleeing governments the U.S. was backing. These asylum denials sparked the Sanctuary Movement, which was modeled after the Underground Railroad. Faith leaders would later come to defy the federal government. They would move thousands of refugees in and out of houses throughout the United States. At the time, more than 500 Protestant, Catholic, and Jewish churches and synagogues participated. At the point of our tragedy and trial, only 26 of 12,000 Salvadoran asylum requests had been granted.

Reverend John Fife worked with Jim Corbett, a Quaker who had a small ranch and thought deeply about faith. Corbett believed the church had failed during the time of the Holocaust, when Jewish people were fleeing danger. He did not want that kind of failure to happen again.

So, he and Reverend Fife began helping people from Central America who were fleeing war and violence. Even though the U.S. government did not want these refugees to stay, the two men felt they had to help. They looked to the past for guidance. In the 1800s, some church members helped enslaved people escape to safety using what was called the Underground Railroad. Fife and Corbett wanted to do something like that again.

Their reason came from Matthew 25:35: *For I was hungry and you gave me something to eat, I was thirsty and you gave me something to drink, I was a stranger and you invited me in.* To them, giving shelter was not just kindness, it was something their faith told them to do.

After a while, they started using the Southside Presbyterian Church in Tucson to temporarily house people fleeing horrific civil wars. In addition to allowing them to sleep at the church, its members provided food, clothing, English lessons, medical care, and access to immigration lawyers.

I was so lucky to meet Reverend John Fife, but at the time, I had no idea how much he and others were doing to help us. What I do remember is walking out of the Pima County Jail onto the parking lot on Twenty-Ninth Street, all thirteen of us who had survived, and seeing hundreds and hundreds of people waiting to welcome us. There were also news agencies present who wanted to cover our story. It was incredibly overwhelming.

Thankfully, the church volunteers had been working on our placement since we arrived at the hospital in Ajo. They quickly ushered us out of the chaos and took us to our host families. I clearly remember meeting my sponsor family. They gave me a warm hug, and I felt welcomed and accepted for the first time in a long while.

I spent a year with the Sanchez family, Marta and Rigoberto, who had two teenage boys and a baby about a year old. They were wonderful people, and I was a good fit in their home because they needed someone to help them. I cooked, cared for the little one, and did all the laundry. Being busy was good for me, and I wanted to contribute rather than be a burden. Marta was involved in the Catholic church, so she and her husband would go on weekend retreats, and I would stay with their three children.

I appreciated their home and didn't go anywhere. I felt secure being in Tucson. We couldn't leave the area until the trial against the smugglers was over. I couldn't continue my journey to my aunt and uncle's home in LA, but that was okay. In the United States, I was safe. I finally felt like I did not have to look over my shoulders. People were friendly to us. I was beginning to find a sense of peace again.

We were interviewed over and over by our lawyers. We

had to relive every minute of the tragedy and remember every detail. I hated that, and I can still feel the pain in my heart from having to describe the terror and torture we experienced. But we did what was required during the trial.

Every day, we sat there facing Felipe, the man who had left us in the desert, and Espinoza, who had lied to us and led many of us to our deaths. They were not being prosecuted for the rape and murder they had committed, only for human smuggling. It was heartbreaking to know there was no justice for the people whose lives had been lost, the people who had become my friends.

It was painful to see the mother of the three daughters who died take the stand. She came over from Los Angeles many times to testify. I know the grueling, year-long trial was incredibly tough on her. During her testimony, she said that she had paid the smugglers to bring her children safely to her, and instead, she was brought the bodies of her three dead daughters.

We were each assigned a lawyer for the trial, who helped us navigate everything. However, as time passed, I could no longer remember much about mine. Years later, when I was giving a presentation for the Tucson Samaritans, a woman came up afterward. "Dora, I have wondered about you for so long, about what happened to you. I follow the Sanctuary Movement and read that someone named Dora would speak, but she had a different last name from yours. Then I read your bio, put two and two together, and knew it was you."

We hugged each other tightly.

"You were my first client, Dora. I was a new graduate with legal aid."

Her name was Suzanna, and alongside her, I also had an advocate, Jim, a social worker, and, of course, Reverend Fife. They had assembled a sizable team of lawyers and others to assist me. It truly took a community, a circle of people who came together with open hearts, each offering their support and strength when I needed it most.

That year was busy with court hearings, interviews with investigators, reporters, and lawyers. And in the midst of it all, my head was full of unanswered questions. Would I be allowed to stay, or would I be deported back to El Salvador, where the civil war was still raging? Young people like me were getting killed every day without justification, just because they were young with a dream. I knew if I went back again, my time and luck would run out. My anxiety rose every time we had a court hearing. Not knowing what would happen was so incredibly upsetting. My nightmares got worse during that time.

Eventually, the trial came to a quiet end. Julio Espinoza and Felipe Vidal both pleaded guilty and were sentenced to five years in a U.S. federal prison. After only a few years, Felipe was pushed from the roof of the prison and killed. Perhaps the cartel silenced him before he could speak of their involvement. We'll never know the full story.

Meanwhile, my fate remained uncertain. However, thanks to a group of pro bono lawyers and dedicated activists who fought for me, I was able to secure a Social Security number, allowing me to work. My first job, which I took with pride, was at McDonald's. I would leave my rundown, one-bedroom trailer at 4:30 a.m. to walk to work, clean the floors, and cook hamburgers.

When I received my first paycheck, I sent money home to help my family. My siblings and mom chose not to leave the country, haunted by my experience in the desert. They did not want to take that same journey, and I did not want them to.

We didn't have phone service at home in El Salvador. My mother, with remarkable patience, would wait for hours in a cramped office just to speak with me. Those calls were filled with heartbreak. We missed each other deeply. When the calls finally connected, my mother and I would often cry together, unable to speak at first. By the time she reached me, it was usually late in the evening.

After the call, she and my siblings would have to walk home through dark, dangerous streets, stepping over pools of blood where people had been killed and left behind on the pavement. They carried a white cloth to inform the officers that they were community members.

The war was brutal on them, and I did everything I could to support my mother and siblings from afar. I left McDonald's for a better job, sewing men's suits in a factory. The job came with benefits, and I enrolled in English classes. While waiting for the bus at 9:30 p.m. after work and school, I would write long letters home. I told my family how much I loved and missed them despite the pain because now I could finally help them.

While trying to build a new life, awaiting my court hearings, and supporting my family, something unexpected yet necessary happened: I reconnected with my father. He came to visit me once in my tiny trailer, but in truth, I was afraid of him. I no longer knew who this man was. He was drunk the entire time, which made the visit feel pointless. I was eager for him to leave and close this chapter of my life.

He returned to Phoenix, where he lived with his new wife, and I never saw him again. He died not long after that. There was no reconciliation, no dramatic ending. And somehow, that was enough.

Chapter Ten

Learning a New Life
Tucson, Arizona, 1982

My high school sweetheart, Andres, came to the States with a Green Card six months after I left for my third attempt. He was living in Los Angeles with his family. We hadn't talked since before I left on my third attempt. He was still in contact with my mom, and she had shared everything that happened to me. Andres was eager to get in touch with me. My mom gave him the phone number of my sponsor family.

One day, I received a phone call. It was Andres. The moment we heard the word *Hola*, we broke down in tears. For the first several minutes, we didn't speak a word, just cried. Once we regained our composure, we spoke for a while about reconnecting as soon as possible. We planned for him to visit me in Tucson within the next month.

Andres came to visit me, and it was as if no time had passed at all. The last time we were together, there were military patrols in our streets. Being together safely in the United States put us both at ease. We had a new outlook on what life could look like, together.

After a few trips to Tucson, Andres moved to be with me. We both worked extremely hard and were able to buy a modest house. It was comforting to have someone who knew my family, my journey, and my first language. My "American Dream" was slowly coming to life. I was safe, married, had a house, and was now pregnant with my first child.

I never imagined that just a couple of summers after

my rescue, I'd be pregnant with my first child. The feeling of carrying a baby was overwhelming and beautiful. It amazed me to think that not long ago, I had come so close to losing my life. And now, I have the chance to give life to someone else.

It was exciting, but I was also very scared. My mother was so far away, and I felt a new layer of loneliness. It was my first child, so many questions ran through my mind. *What would he look like? Would it be a boy or a girl? Would the baby resemble me, his father, or someone else entirely? Or would he come out looking like E.T.?*

The whole experience felt surreal, how life had flipped so dramatically from nearly dying to now, just six months away from holding my beautiful baby boy, Eric.

Life was turning a page once again. Eight months after giving birth, I got my residency through Andres. When you come to this country undocumented, you have to ask for forgiveness when you change your status to get a green card. We had to take my letter asking for forgiveness to an ambassador at a U.S. Embassy in another country. Unable to go to El Salvador because of the active civil war, we had to choose where we could go, and the ambassador of that country would determine if the United States would let me in, a bizarre process.

The three of us took the trip to Calgary, Canada, a place I knew little about—especially when it came to snow. I had never experienced a frigid cold before. Growing up in El Salvador and now living in Tucson, Arizona, I was used to warm weather year-round. We boarded the plane in thin jackets, completely unprepared for what was waiting on the other side. As soon as the airplane doors opened, the cold hit us like a wall. I remember looking at my poor baby as his eyes grew wide and his nose turned bright red. The new experiences never seemed to end.

The trip was short. The next day, I had my green card appointment at the U.S. Embassy. I arrived early, filled with nervous energy and hope. This was a big moment. One step closer to finally becoming a U.S. citizen. Just two days later, we were flying back home. But this time, I returned as a U.S. green card holder.

Before receiving my green card, I lived cautiously. I worked, cared for my son, and tried not to draw attention to myself. I was always worried that one wrong step could mean losing everything. But after that moment in Calgary, something shifted. With more security, I felt free to step beyond survival.

I began volunteering and supporting housing efforts for asylum seekers. The humanitarian aid organizations would call me, saying, "Dora, we have a family that needs housing." I would take them into my home for a few months until they were settled. I knew I would never turn my back on people enduring what I had gone through. We were connected through our experiences and shared trauma. I was able to go from someone who was saved from the desert to being someone who saved others from the desert.

Tucson, my second home, has now become the place I've lived the longest, even longer than El Salvador. The love and hospitality I've found here have shaped my life in ways I never could have imagined. I often ask myself, *How can I not give back when I've been embraced by a community that continues to lift others without hesitation?*

One of my most vivid memories is of the first family I sponsored through Southside Presbyterian Church, who were from Guatemala. The little boy, Baidito, is now in his forties, but I can still picture him at just four years old. I had recently taught myself to drive, and I remember arriving nervously at the Welcome Center to meet them.

His mother, Patricia, stood in the parking lot, wearing an

ankle-length dress, her long black hair falling down her back. She held tightly to Baidito's small hand while her husband, Baidan, stood beside them, carrying a see-through plastic bag that contained everything they owned. That moment stayed with me, not just because of what they carried but because of the strength and dignity they showed, even in such uncertainty.

I wasn't doing this work alone. Andres supported our decision to host families. Like me, he was from El Salvador and knew firsthand the importance of showing up for others. We had grown up together, more friends than anything, and we shared a deep bond through our Catholic faith and a sense of duty to care for those in need. When Andres joined the Marine Corps, our lives changed. He came back different, carrying burdens I couldn't always reach. Slowly, we drifted apart, and eventually, we divorced.

Still, I often wonder how things might have unfolded if I, or anyone in our group, had been granted asylum. But in the 1980s, that was almost unheard of, especially for people from Guatemala and El Salvador. The U.S. wouldn't admit its responsibility as people reached points of desperation where they had no option but to flee. I carried a great deal of shame during this time in my life for coming to the U.S. undocumented. It would take years of working with the Sanctuary Movement to fully understand the conditions I suffered under and that I had no choice. There is no shame in seeking safety.

Each of us took a different path to secure our citizenship. Like me, some got married. When amnesty was introduced in 1986, many survivors of my group, including myself, took care of their paperwork accordingly. I can't speak for everyone, but I had a clear case for asylum under international law. The challenge, however, was the United States' refusal to acknowledge its involvement in El Salvador and other

Central American countries at the time. The U.S. aligned itself with governments in those countries as political allies in the fight against communism, but it turned a blind eye to the persecution that their people were facing, including me.

Today, many reasons people flee their countries, such as economic collapse, environmental crises, or the inability to find work to feed their families, are not valid grounds for asylum. A country's financial crisis doesn't count. If people can't grow crops because of drought, or if rising sea levels submerge their land, asylum law has no provision for them. These realities are only getting worse. The question remains: Will the government ever take responsibility for these changes?

As a citizen, I now visit the border every week to assist families seeking asylum. I meet with them during the most vulnerable moments of their lives, whether it's women, men, or children. Despite everything they've endured and all that lies ahead, they are thankful to have arrived on American soil. They are not sneaking across the desert to trek through it like I did, but their journey is often just as dangerous. Many arrive only to be separated from their families and placed in detention centers.

The factors that shaped my journey are still relevant to the people I meet today. Yet, the system refuses to acknowledge the broader global challenges pushing people to seek refuge. It's a contradiction that continues to shape the lives of many, and I am left wondering every day whether the government will ever catch up to the realities of so many.

Santa Ana, El Salvador - Age 10.
Taken a year after I began working in the coffee fields at age nine.

Santa Ana, El Salvador - 1976.
Crowned queen of the soccer team at Colegio San Lorenzo, Catholic high school.

"Yo no soy político, no soy sociólogo, no soy economista, pero como pastor me toca construir la verdadera Iglesia de Nuestro Señor Jesucristo".

(Homilía 25/04/79)

San Salvador, El Salvador – March 24, 1980.
The church where Archbishop Óscar Romero was assassinated. His homily from exactly one year earlier called on soldiers to stop the violence. That message changed everything.

Organ Pipe Cactus National Monument, Arizona – July 1980.
A national magazine captured this scene as Border Patrol tried to revive me. I survived. Many didn't.

Juanita
age 12

*The three sisters who died during our desert crossing.
I carry their memory with me always.*

Inés
age 14

Alicia
age 16

(pseudonyms)

Organ Pipe Cactus National Monument, Arizona – July 1980.
I collapsed from heatstroke and dehydration. This photo was taken as I was being airlifted to safety.

Organ Pipe Cactus National Monument, Arizona – July 2023.
I return each year to honor the thirteen lives lost during our desert crossing.

Sasabe, Sonora, Mexico – 2021.
Gail and I visiting the center for the first time. This would later become Casa de la Esperanza, a shelter for migrants in crisis.

Sasabe, Sonora, Mexico – 2022.
Casa de la Esperanza, a place of safety, dignity, and rest for those on their journey toward the "American Dream."

Tucson, Arizona – April 2015.
Our wedding day. Walking arm in arm with David, ready to begin this next chapter together.

Lake Coatepeque, El Salvador – 2021.
I was visiting my mom on what became our last trip together. She passed two weeks later.

Phoenix, Arizona – March 2023.
With my children at my daughter Anna's wedding. A moment I never imagined I'd live to see. Left to right: Trever (33), Javier (35), me, Anna (32), Cynthia (34), and Eric (42).

Tucson, Arizona - Present day.
With my four grandchildren: Elijah, Alena, Warren, and Solomon. They are my whole world.

Chapter Eleven

From Motherhood to Me

Tucson, Arizona, 2011

There are many parts of my life that I've chosen to skip over, not because they weren't beautiful, challenging, and full of stories to share, but because this book is meant to be the story of my transformation and resilience. It is the story of my heart, the heart of my people, and the strength we all possess to rise above hard times and do good in the world.

Over two decades have passed since the events I've already shared, and much has changed along the way. While I don't dive into every detail of my life as a mother, my five beautiful children are at the core of my existence. They are my lifeline and my hope for the future. They've made me a mother and grandmother. Though their stories are theirs to tell, their presence has shaped every step of mine.

Equally important are the chapters of my life where I found purpose in humanitarian work. Helping others has been a central thread in my journey, shaping my understanding of what it means to rise above adversity.

In the years that followed, my children and I moved all over the state. By 2011, I decided to return to Tucson. Some of my children were about to start college at the University of Arizona and Northern Arizona University, and the rest were moving out to begin their careers and pursue independence. It was a lonely time for me, a time of transition.

My children leaving home was one of the most difficult

times in my life. They always gave me a reason to get up in the morning and keep going. In 1992, I sponsored my mother for a green card, and she was eventually granted one. From then on, she would live with us for six months out of the year, and she continued this even after my children had all left by 2012. Caring for her helped ease that shift.

My children are very close to one another, despite a seven-year age gap between my oldest and the next one. They love and respect each other. I have never seen them have a big fight or heated conversation. If there is a disagreement, they love each other unconditionally, allowing any issue to be discussed and resolved.

All of my children believe deeply in human rights and my work. They support those in need and have tender hearts. As the years go by, my children are building their own lives and families, making it harder for us to find time to come together. Now, any time we can manage to gather feels like my "Thanksgiving." I am grateful when we're all in one place, regardless of the date. A weekend in September? No problem.

When we're together, it's a celebration. That's when I cook their favorite foods. *Panes con pavo* is always the most requested dish, but they also ask, "Mom, can you cook your Salvadoran turkey?" So, of course, I do that too.

After I had been back in Tucson for several months, a friend of mine asked me if I had heard from a mutual past coworker, David. David had been a friend from our days working together in social services, but we had lost touch over time. I said, "No, how's he doing?" She shared that he had just ended a relationship and that his father had passed away. Knowing David had never been married and had no children, I imagined this was a difficult time for him.

I decided to reach out and call, leaving a message: "Hey, this is Dora. I'm back in Tucson. I hope you're doing well."

Five minutes passed, and I got a phone call back. He said in a giddy voice, "Oh, I wasn't going to let that call go unanswered."

We connected and caught up on what had been happening in our lives, with our families, and everything that had passed since we last saw each other. At the end of our call, I asked, "Do you want to get together for coffee or lunch?"

We noticed that our friendship was still very strong. David and I are a good match as he is a good listener, and I am a great talker. I noticed that David balanced me. I'm a total extrovert. I enjoy being in social groups, while David is much more reserved.

When we met for lunch, I had so much to tell him. I began with a story about my long years with my second husband, my divorce, and my adventures with my children, who are now young adults. That poor guy listened for hours.

Over a couple of months, we would meet for coffee and lunch, and then he eventually invited me on a date to the movies. I cherished his company. I enjoyed his calm personality. So loving and respectful.

As we spent more time together, I introduced David to my children. They all fell immediately in love with him. Some of them remembered him from when we worked together ten years prior. They said, "Oh, we remember this guy. He's nice."

I was still naïve about us, thinking it was just a nice friendship. But I knew it was much more than that as I started to feel those deeper emotions: missing him, a giddy feeling when he texted, a desire to call David, and a sense of hopefulness as I anticipated his next call.

As my five children began to start new chapters in their lives, I found myself alone after being in a busy home with my kids and my mother for so many years. It was a tough feeling, this loneliness. I knew I still had the love of my children, but it was not the same. My mother had returned to El Salvador, and I was now alone in my home for the first time. I no longer had anyone to serve breakfast to or share laughter and stories over dinner. Life had changed so drastically in such a short amount of time.

So, when David started filling in those gaps, I thought, *Oh my goodness, he could become an incredible partner.* About six months later, we became romantic. I had those tickling butterflies in my stomach. I never thought I would have them again. After you have been through a great deal and no longer trust in love, it is a delight to find it again.

So one day I joked with him and said, "Listen, if you think we're going to have any sort of a relationship, you'd better move forward, because we're old. I don't want you to propose to me when I am in a wheelchair." We laughed, and I thought that would be the end of it.

Months later, David and I took a family trip to visit my son, Javier, who lives in California. We took my mother, who was back in the U.S., and visited with my *Tia* Pacita in Los Angeles. Every time I visited my *Tia* Pacita, I couldn't help but think about how I was supposed to get on a bus to be with her, but ended up in such a tragic situation. It brought me closure, being able to visit her now whenever I wanted.

We visited Cabrito Beach on a spectacular, clear, sunny day and bought food for a picnic lunch. When my mother, aunt, and Javier settled in for a nap under the shade of a tree, David invited me to go for a stroll with him. We walked across the sand to a large rock and climbed up on top. The waves were pounding the rocks, crashing up against them.

I noticed him getting funny, but I never imagined why. He got on one knee and asked me to marry me traditionally, holding a ring in a little box.

I said, "Oh my God, what are you doing? You want to marry me? Oh, David, this is wild. We're old."

He laughed. "That's why I'm asking you."

"Yes!" I tugged him to stand up and held him close. "Yes," I whispered to him.

Later, I told the rest of my children and there were tears of joy. We were all filled with happiness.

Javier was thrilled. He was the last child to leave home and always felt a responsibility to care for me. Now, Javier could experience life fully and knew that his mother had someone who would now care for her.

Chapter Twelve

Turning Healing Into Purpose

I entered this new chapter as a married woman. Though it was my third marriage, this one felt different in every way. David filled the loneliness that came with being an empty nester and gave me the true partnership I had longed for, yet something still felt missing. I continued working full-time as a social worker while caring for my mom during her stay. Once her six-month visit ended, I didn't suddenly have a lot of free time, but I had just enough space in my life to want to give some of it back. So I reached out to friends in the humanitarian world to see where I might be able to volunteer.

I attended a Tucson Samaritans meeting one Tuesday night, hoping to see where I could help. Unknowingly, I was reconnected with Reverend John Fife. Across the room, I saw his big smile as I approached him. Extending his arms out for a hug, he happily said, "Dora, it is always an honor to see you. How happy I am to see you here." I have such a deep admiration for him. I will always be grateful for the countless lives he and so many others saved from the horrible wars in El Salvador, Guatemala, and Nicaragua.

As we began to catch up, I shared my reason for attending the meeting: "I want to sign up to volunteer. Let me know what I can do to help." With the same big grin, Reverend John Fife responded, "Well, if that's the case, grab a set of keys to one of the volunteer trucks, and go to the desert and look for people." I was surprised by his response and how uncomplicated the task was.

The following Saturday, I went on my first Samaritan volunteer trip. The plan for the day was to head out to the desert to clean up belongings left behind by people risking everything in search of safety and a better life.

Alongside me was Alma, a fellow Samaritan and one of the kindest souls I'd ever met. With a beautiful smile and a calm, steady presence, Alma moved through the desert with care, picking up water bottles, clothing, and other scattered belongings.

We opened the barbed wire to emerge into the desert and begin cleaning. As I bent over to pick up an abandoned shoe, I couldn't help but wonder: was this person alive, with their family, or had they lost their life to the desert?

On our drive home, I felt an immense sense of fulfillment and connection. I knew I was on the cusp of finding my greater purpose.

The years passed, and I continued volunteering steadily with the Tucson Samaritans. It was now 2016, which meant we were in the middle of a new presidential election. One day, I was sitting on the couch watching the news. The Republican candidate stood at a podium, name-calling people who look like me, who share similar stories, the most derogatory names. I felt a rush of rage and anger. I was sick of people looking down at me, at us, not understanding the journeys I had once made or the ones others were still making.

Until this point in my life, I never really shared my personal story with anyone about how I came to the U.S. Maybe I felt a slight amount of shame or embarrassment. I held it close to my heart to protect my kids from knowing the details of my traumatic journey, and also in a way to protect myself from having to relive it.

The rhetoric toward people seeking asylum, anyone who was portrayed as "other," was becoming nastier. I kept thinking, *if only people knew the realities behind these stories. If only they heard my story, they might feel more compassion.* It was time for me to speak out and advocate for all those making the journey toward a better life. I have always believed that storytelling can change people's hearts and minds. How I would do this was uncertain, but at this moment, I felt inspired.

The goal was to share my story and raise awareness among those uninformed about the experiences of migrants, hoping they would see them as humans who want a second chance at life. The Consulate of El Salvador was hosting an event for the community. I decided to attend in hopes of networking and meeting fellow Salvadorans in Tucson.

Once I arrived, I immediately felt like a piece of home was nearby. The Consul General delivered a speech of encouragement and positivity, acknowledging that the community was concerned about the political climate. I admired him and his kindness in the way he spoke.

I introduced myself to the group and quickly found that there was a real opportunity to get involved, just the kind of involvement I had been hoping for. I learned that the Consul General and some volunteers had founded a small non-profit organization, *Salvavision Rescue Arizona.* They were helping Salvadorans who had recently arrived in the U.S. through asylum and also supporting people who had been deported back to El Salvador.

I began to volunteer and loved every minute of it. We would organize clothing drives, host parties for families assisted through the consulate, and raise funds to support individuals in El Salvador. The passion within me took over, and I slowly assumed a leading position in the group.

It was far from easy to plan and execute everything we wanted to do with Salvavision Rescue Arizona. I had many ideas about how we could help people, but the time commitment was heavy. The group grew hesitant about how ambitious the project was becoming, and one by one, members began to dissolve.

When I met with the General, he shared that Salvavision Rescue Arizona was never meant to become large, and there were no plans to continue growing. He must have seen the disappointment in my face as he turned to me and said, "Dora, have you ever thought about starting your own nonprofit organization? You would be great at it." That was the first time someone had asked me that. I never considered that to be an option. He continued, "You don't need a lot of people to start. Lean on your family, and the rest will fall into place."

Later that night, I spoke with Anna, my youngest daughter. She loves helping others as much as I do, but she's also a realist. I shared with her that Salvavision Rescue Arizona was dissolving, and I was considering creating my own organization.

Being involved with the Samaritans and now Salvavision Rescue Arizona, I realized there was much work to do. I shared with Anna my dream of helping people, not just in Tucson, but all over the world. After a long pause, Anna replied with excitement, "Mom, I've been waiting for this day. Let's get started."

I was committed to continuing the work that Salvavision Rescue Arizona did. With my sleeves rolled up and the support of my husband, children, and fellow volunteers, I became the director of my own nonprofit, *Salvavision.*

Chapter Thirteen

You Are Not Alone

A few years later, Salvavision's mission had taken shape: to walk alongside migrants and asylum seekers, meeting their needs on both sides of the border and offering hope where systems had failed. Immigration policies were tightening, and the U.S. government's approach to asylum seekers was becoming more restrictive. People were being turned away at the border, detained in overcrowded facilities, and left with limited access to legal support.

In response to these challenges, Salvavision stepped in to provide the assistance that was desperately needed. This was the first time I was leading this work through my own nonprofit, and the urgency of the moment was undeniable.

During this period, the urgent need for community support was overwhelming. I began volunteering inside detention facilities and became involved with *No More Deaths*, specifically their legal collective, *Keep Tucson Together*. A bilingual lawyer from the group recruited me to help. I worked alongside them, translating for detained immigrants, refugees, and asylum seekers who needed legal support but had no voice in a system stacked against them.

Each week, my routine became a blur of visits to detention centers across southern Arizona. After spending hours there, I'd load up my car with boxes of donated supplies and drive across the border to migrant shelters in Nogales, Mexico. My trunk overflowed with boxes of toys, hygiene items, clothes, and shoes, small things that brought comfort and dignity to people who had lost almost everything.

One of the places I visited regularly was the La Palma Correctional Center in Eloy, Arizona, which is run by the private prison giant CoreCivic. There, I joined other volunteers to meet with detainees, listen to their stories, and write down their experiences. We took down every detail. We weren't lawyers, but we played a critical role. We passed our notes along to immigration lawyers who would then sift through the cases and determine who had a shot at asylum. Our work helped them move the process forward, allowing them to spend less time on paperwork and more time fighting for justice.

The thing that haunted me most was hearing how many of the detainees had come to the port of entry seeking asylum, only to be met not with protection, but with prison. Separated from their spouses and children, they suffered inhumane conditions. The generational trauma we continue to inflict on families who are seeking safety and a better life is devastating, and we will all continue to feel the repercussions from these actions.

When I met with them, I always told them, "You are not alone. You have an army behind you. You don't know that, but you do. That's why we do this together."

In Florence, Arizona, another facility, a federal prison, held asylum seekers with prior entry attempts or time previously spent in the U.S. Once they were inside, they were cut off. Even our best immigration attorneys couldn't reach them. These people, who had fled violence, who were desperately seeking refuge, were being treated like criminals. Their only "crime" was trying to survive.

Then came the pandemic.

When COVID-19 hit, face-to-face visits were suspended. The federal administration suspended all social visits to

Immigration and Customs Enforcement detention centers, meaning that those inside were cut off from all face-to-face visits. Detainees were trapped in overcrowded housing units, 150 people at a time, with no ability to distance, no protection, and little medical care. Many got sick and did not survive.

With the loss of in-person contact, I knew I had to do something to keep their spirits alive, so I launched a letter-writing campaign. I wanted to be sure the people detained inside didn't feel forgotten. I continued answering their calls, up to twenty a day. Not knowing if this would be the last call they would ever make, I felt I needed to take each call. I always said the same thing over and over, "You are not alone. We are here."

The biggest challenge we had was bonds.

Ten thousand dollars. Thirty thousand dollars. Where were they supposed to find that kind of money? Even volunteers and humanitarian workers in the U.S. didn't have that kind of cash. It felt impossible. And yet, this is the price of freedom in a system that holds people hostage in exchange for their release.

But we didn't give up. We poured our time, energy, and resources into collective efforts to bring some humanity into this broken system. What keeps me going is knowing that I am not alone in this. I do this with a community. I would never be able to do this alone. We were able to raise the funds and gain freedom for many people with the support of a large organization called the National Bond Fund – Freedom for Immigrants.

We eventually raised the money to help so many people get out of detention. The highest bond we raised was $50,000. It was for a father of four teenagers. His only "crime" was crossing the desert twice to try to reunite with his children, all of whom are U.S. citizens. The bond was huge, but we made it happen. The lowest bond we raised was $3,000, which was still a lot for many people.

During the summer of 2020, David, my youngest son, Trever, and I joined a caravan of over one hundred vehicles and drove to the detention center in Eloy, Arizona. We gathered in a nearby parking lot, each car decorated with signs: "Free Them All," "Compassion Is Not a Crime," "You Are Not Forgotten." We stayed in our cars or stood outside, masked and spaced apart, but united in purpose. People brought drums, pots and pans, and air horns. We made as much noise as we could.

We circled the detention center. Over and over. Honking, shouting, hoping, praying that someone inside would hear us. And they did.

A Nicaraguan young man I had been helping inside called me, "¡Dorita! We hear everyone!" My heart cracked wide open. At that moment, those words reminded me why we continue to show up. Even when it feels like no one's watching. Even when it feels like nothing is changing. We show up anyway.

It wasn't just noise. It was proof. Proof that they were not alone. That someone cared. That someone remembered they were in there.

Later that night, people inside said they could hear us chanting for over an hour. Some stood at the windows, waving. Others banged back on the walls. It didn't change their situation overnight, but it reminded them and us that the community can reach across walls, fences, and razor wire.

That caravan was one of the most powerful things I've ever been part of. It brought together people of all backgrounds, people who didn't know what to do, but knew they had to do something. And together, we did.

Chapter Fourteen

The Birth of Casa de la Esperanza
Sasabe, Sonora, Mexico

By the Fall of 2020, my work stretched across both sides of the border, from U.S. detention centers to the streets of small Mexican border towns. That September, I traveled to Sasabe, Sonora, Mexico, a place I had only heard about until then. Salvavision's work had mostly focused on Nogales and Sonoyta, but this time I went with another humanitarian, Gail Kocourek, to deliver donations to migrants stranded with no resources.

When we arrived, we went straight to a smuggler's stash house, dropping off bags of clothing and other donations. Gail knew to go there because she was aware people had been deported with no choice but to turn to the smugglers for another chance to cross.

As we drove away, I told Gail, "I saw men taking videos of us."

"Oh, they always do that. You'll get used to it."

For me, it was a scary experience. I never wanted to go back there. I never wanted to 'get used' to being videotaped. However, I soon discovered that this town, with a population of approximately 2,500, was facing a significant crisis.

During the COVID-19 pandemic, the administration instituted Title 42, an emergency health policy that required all asylum seekers and migrants apprehended in the United States to be returned to Mexico immediately to protect the health of U.S. citizens. It was a policy that made the lives of the Border Patrol much more manageable and the lives of others much more tragic.

The Border Patrol could round up everyone who was crossing without allowing them to tell their story. There was no asylum, no chance of asking for safety. There was no due process, and why they sought help did not matter. Migrants were being gathered up and sent to border towns in Mexico, including Sasabe. All those seeking asylum were deported to remote border towns, whether they had begun their journey there or not, and most had not.

Sasabe, Sonora, lacks transportation for locals, a hospital, and shelters. The closest services are seventy miles away in Altar, Sonora. Border Patrol had started dropping off about 150 migrants per day in this small town with nowhere to go, leaving hundreds of people vulnerable, including women and children, with no resources to determine what would happen next in their journeys. Their dignity and rights were stripped from them.

I learned this was happening, and my fellow volunteers and I began showing up and bringing what we could. We began delivering essential aid to these stranded individuals, including water, food, blankets, and other necessities. We wanted to show them that they mattered and that there are people who care about them. I wanted them to feel how I felt 40 years ago, when communities started to rally behind me, recognizing me as a human being who deserves respect and the chance at a safe life.

When we were in town that first day delivering aid, the director of *Grupos Beta* saw us handing out clothing and food to migrants returning across the border. He called us in for a meeting. *Grupos Beta de Protección a Migrantes* is a Mexican government organization designed to assist migrants throughout the country. It was me, Gail, and another fellow volunteer, Sister Judy. We thought we were in trouble, three older gals going to the principal's office. We weren't sure what the director would say: 'Who are you? What are you doing?' or if he would ask us for money to help with the situation.

Partway through the meeting, Sister Judy leaned over, and I heard her translate for Gail in a whisper, "He's not asking for money. He's asking for help." We were blown away. He provided us with space in their building to set up tables. He had been struggling with this situation since March.

Gail, who had been visiting Sasabe regularly as a volunteer, had not returned since the start of the pandemic. She was shocked to see what had been happening with the deportations.

We promptly acted upon his support request. We enlisted Salvavision and other sister organizations, such as *Tucson Samaritans, Green Valley-Sahuarita Samaritans, Humane Borders, No More Deaths,* and tireless, committed individuals nationwide. No one could understand what was happening. It was unlike anything any of us had seen. We all came out to help day after day, month after month.

We provided services on the street at the border crossing station. We set up tables and brought large urns of coffee, which were nice and hot. As the weather turned cold, we brought jackets, blankets, and closed-toe shoes.

Every week, we delivered 700 individual bags of food. Each one held a fruit cup, a protein bar, a chicken sandwich, and a bottle of water, all lovingly packed by a small team of volunteers, including my oldest daughter, Cynthia, and even my three-year-old grandson, their little hands helping in my garage back in Tucson. It was a labor of love, a family effort that reminded me that compassion starts at home.

We would cross the port of entry into Mexico and set up our tables, waiting for the buses to begin unloading confused and traumatized people. Each day, the number of buses and people continued to increase. It felt like an endless flow of dazed and confused individuals and families.

A caravan of volunteers made the hour-and-a-half drive from Tucson about three times a week or more. We did this every week for months, all the way through the winter. The temperatures were cold, averaging in the 40s. We were cold ourselves, standing outside, huddled against the wall, handing out donations.

It was heartbreaking to see migrants in these conditions, with mothers and tiny children, some just newborns, sleeping on the streets. Many were Indigenous from Guatemala and didn't speak Spanish or English. This was all during the pandemic, which limited the number of volunteers available to do this humanitarian work.

Each day, regardless of how big or small our volunteer group was, we knew the stranded people relied on our help to survive. When you have an adult man standing face to face with you, crying like a child, freezing because they took everything he owned, leaving him in just a t-shirt with no shoelaces in his shoes, no belt to hold up his pants, it keeps you working through your discomfort and coming back day after day. These are people. How has that been lost on so many?

The number of migrants being deported to this tiny town continued to grow. At one point, we were seeing more than 700 people a week. There seemed to be no slowing down. It was criminal. It was not okay. You do not take hundreds and hundreds of people seeking asylum from all over the world and just dump them anytime, day or night, in a town with inadequate resources to care for them, absolutely no way for them to find safety. Why were the governments on either side not stepping up to help?

These were Mexican nationals and people from Honduras, Guatemala, El Salvador, and many other countries. They did not know where they had been deported to. They were stranded and had no idea where to go or what to do. Gangs and government officials took most of their belongings along the way. And while they had lost everything, their most precious loss was their dignity.

We started doing a lot of work to bring this issue to light. We needed Americans to be aware of what was happening to all these women, children, families, and men seeking help and freedom. First, our friend Ryan from *The Intercept* came and wrote an article, which helped. Next, we brought in *NPR*, which also helped.

"We have to reach more people. Who knows anyone at *The New York Times?*" I asked. One of our volunteers mentioned she had a connection there and would reach out. They were interested in the story, and the journalist was in Sasabe with a photographer within two days.

I was on the front page of *The New York Times* for the second time in my life. Over 40 years later, after my tragedy in 1980, this felt like a full-circle moment. Within four days of the story being published on December 14, 2020, the number of people being deported to Sasabe dropped from 150 a day to 30 or 40. It was incredible and quite sudden. We saw firsthand the power of attention and awareness in action.

We weren't asking the Border Patrol to change the law, just to reroute people to towns with the services to help them survive. At the heart of it, we believed that every person deserved to be treated with dignity and respect. Yet, despite receiving a share of the $19.6 billion in annual funding for Customs and Border Protection, the Border Patrol told us they didn't have the resources to move people to places ready to support them. It was disheartening, a painful reminder of how easily humanity can get lost in bureaucracy.

We saw how quickly that shifted with a bit of media attention. If they have the money to build the "super wall," they have the money to care for people humanely.

We continued to deliver meals, clothing, and assistance even as the number of people sent to Sasabe declined. By the end of December, the director of *Grupos Beta* approached us again, saying he wanted to show us some empty houses in town. He asked if we had ever considered establishing a place in Sasabe to assist people.

I laughed inside, thinking, *He must think we have money because that's a big commitment.* However, I have never been afraid to say yes, so I went with him to take a look. After seeing those houses, he brought us to one final place on the way back to the port of entry.

I fell in love with it immediately. I first noticed it was completely fenced in with a gate, making it more secure and private. It was on the corner, across from a military office, making it visible but safe. It was perfect. Being a couple of blocks from the port of entry, people who were deported would only need to walk straight down the road.

The director gave us the owner's phone number, and I called that day. I told him who I was and what we were doing. He said, "Yes, I've seen all the work you have been doing in the town. I like what you are accomplishing."

He owned most of the few stores in the area and was a kind man who showed real compassion. We agreed that someone would meet us at the building the next day, and with that plan in place, we made yet another trip down to Sasabe.

As his assistant opened the doors, we went in and could see how perfect it was. It used to be a restaurant, which still had the tables, chairs, booths, and benches. It was beautiful inside, with an amazing kitchen toward the back of the building. The assistant said, "Well, you'll like this too. It has a shower." I blurted out, "What? Are you serious?"

Gail was so excited. "This is it, an answer to our prayers."

Her shiny white hair and broad grin seemed to glow with the possibilities.

When we asked the owner how much rent he wanted, he replied that he wanted $500 per month. I told him that we are a donations-based group and that Gail and I didn't have money to pay personally. He reduced the rent to $400, and we shook hands.

Next, we called the town's commissioner, who agreed to meet with us. She asked us to write a proposal about opening a resource center in Sasabe that she could present to the *presidente*, her boss.

My daughter, Anna, is my right-hand person in logistics for Salvavision, and I began brainstorming how to word it. We focused on explaining that the center would support the entire Sasabe community, not just our migrant brothers and sisters. It would be a resource center, not a shelter.

We highlighted how the community had been struggling with the constant influx of people being sent back from the United States. We emphasized that the center would also be a place for the community to call their own, a space where they could hold activities and celebrate *bautismos, quinceañeras,* and whatever else they wanted.

A week later, I brought the proposal to the commissioner. Just a few days after that, I received a text: "Dorita, we're good to go." I was overjoyed. From that moment on, we hit the ground running. Gail and I drove down every day to clean and prepare the space. We had no time to waste.

Through our networks and social media, we posted we needed more volunteers to run the center and supplies to fill the space. Dozens of volunteers responded to the call and were as excited as we were to support our dream. The transformation had begun.

I had never stepped into a small Mexican border community

in this way before. I understood that we needed to respect the people who call Sasabe home and be cautious not to disturb their way of life. We were there to enhance things, not cause trouble.

It took some time for the community in Sasabe to trust us. Who were we, and what were we doing there? Could we really be there to offer help and support?

One by one, women from Sasabe began to step forward. They wanted to be involved. At first, I didn't think the volunteers would come from the town, but through Salvavision, we raised enough money to pay them to manage the center five days a week. It was a relief, as I knew that Gail, our volunteers, and I couldn't commit to being there every day.

We began to form bonds and friendships with these women. It will always be one of the highlights of my life, the connection to this community, and the relationships I saw formed among the women and families. I know we were all changed in ways that continue to unfold.

In those early days of visiting Sasabe, I learned a lot about honoring the flow of the community and the hierarchy present in border towns. The way people moved through the town, with whom they interacted, and how they respected the unspoken rules became clear over time. I understood that it wasn't just about providing aid, it was about respecting the local culture, the relationships, and the dynamics that existed in Sasabe.

The smugglers moving migrants across the border were mainly part of the cartel, and also residents of the town. They were the brothers, sons, and husbands of the families I was getting to know and becoming close with.

All I wanted to do was continue to help those being deported to Sasabe. They needed a place to regain a sense of humanity and dignity. Most of the people who were apprehended crossing the desert or when asking for asylum had been returned to Mexico after days without showers or enough food and water. Their feet were destroyed from blisters.

Many people had issues with diabetes, high blood pressure, and dehydration, and their medications had been taken from them when they were apprehended. We needed to create a corner in the center to triage all the medical needs. They needed a place to rest and recover from the journey they had just taken. I always say that Salvavision was created to help put out fires, and this one felt enormous.

Our mission in Sasabe began as a response to a crisis created by the United States government, but it turned into something extraordinary. We finally opened the doors after six months of preparation, seeking financial donations and gathering items needed to supply the center.

Casa de la Esperanza resource center officially opened on May 1, 2021.

It was a day of celebration! We invited people from town to join us in a small ribbon-cutting ceremony and had a piñata for the children to enjoy.

In the lead-up to the opening, many of us, as volunteers, held panels with humanitarian organizations to share the news of this amazing new resource. We also had community discussions in Sasabe and sent information about the center to officials on both sides of the border. The center received financial help from grants and many private donors nationwide.

While many organizations collaborated to pull this project together, it would be operated through Salvavision. There was a lot of excitement. The opening was beautiful to watch, and we knew we could manage the center's workload with the reduced number of deportees. We could make a difference in the lives of those making the journey to safety.

Humane Borders, an incredible organization in Tucson that has been placing water in the desert for migrants for over twenty years, wanted to help in a big way. They generously agreed to cover the first month's rent for Casa de la Esperanza and continued to support it every month thereafter. It was hard to believe that it had already been eight months since we made that first trip to Sasabe. What we accomplished during that time was impressive.

Two days after the grand opening, I flew to El Salvador to visit my mother and siblings. My mom had initially planned to return to the United States in March to enjoy the spring weather and the desert wildflowers, which was her favorite time of year. However, the Salvadoran government canceled her flight multiple times due to the pandemic. They were not letting people leave easily.

On that May trip, I spent two beautiful weeks with my mother. We enjoyed breakfast together, took long walks, talked about everything, and looked at old pictures. It was almost as if we knew it would be our last time together. That moment will forever live in my heart, a quiet moment of connection as we walked together on the beach, the waves rolling in beside us.

Once I returned from my trip, my daughter, Anna, got engaged. We FaceTimed with my mom at the engagement party to share the happy news. The excitement of a family wedding in our future and the thought of my mom being able to attend made us all happy.

The following week, my mother passed away. During the night, she had a stroke, and when my sister, who lived with her, found her in bed with a weak pulse, *Mamá* was rushed to the hospital. She had her health issues, but we never thought she would go this way. My sister called me, and I got on the next flight to El Salvador.

As I was in the air to be by her side, she took her last breath. The two weeks we had spent together offered invaluable healing for me, and I was able to find some peace around her dying because of that last special time we had together.

When I returned from my mother's funeral, I resumed work on creating the special place that Casa de la Esperanza was becoming. The center began to see a steady flow of people at our front door. Showers, a hot meal from our kitchen, a change of clothing, hygiene items, phone calls to family members, and legal aid through a fellow humanitarian organization were available to anyone who came to our door.

More and more attention was paid to our work, sparking the interest of people from all over who wanted to contribute. I knew we had an opportunity to aid those presenting at our center and contribute back to the town of Sasabe. A team of retired doctors and nurses from the Tucson area learned that Sasabe had only one doctor for its 2,500 people. They began visiting twice a month to provide medical assistance.

While this was great, having consistent medical care in Sasabe was the ultimate goal. As a result, we formed a partnership with the Southeast Arizona Health Education Center (SEAHEC), which helped provide scholarships to local women in Sasabe to attend nursing school in Hermosillo, Sonora, Mexico.

Casa de la Esperanza was a place of healing. People would show up at the center with all their belongings stuffed into a small trash bag, a practice adopted by the U.S. Border Patrol. Exhausted from whatever journey they had just encountered, you would always see this expression of relief as folks entered the center. I'll never forget when a woman from Guatemala came out of the shower with fresh clothes and started combing her beautiful, long, black hair. It was heartwarming to witness the sliver of dignity these people were regaining in these moments. They felt like people again.

You could see it in their eyes.

In addition to going to Sasabe, Mexico, I delivered hand sanitizer, food, clothing, and shoes to support the shelters in Nogales, Agua Prieta, and Sonoyta. The pandemic continued to be a significant concern, making our humanitarian work even more challenging. From March 2020, when Title 42 was enacted, until May 2023, when it was rescinded, the United States expelled 2.8 million people.

Chapter Fifteen

False Promises & Closed Doors

This work allowed me to meet people from all across the globe, including Africa, Haiti, Russia, India, the Dominican Republic, and the Mediterranean. There was also a large number of people coming from the Middle East. Many attempted to cross through Lukeville, Arizona, only to find themselves in the same desert where my journey had almost ended tragically.

When they were apprehended, they were deported to Nogales, Mexico, about five hours away. It felt as though the U.S. government did this intentionally to put distance between the expelled migrants and any support system they might have had waiting for them in Mexico.

Even one worker from *Grupos Beta*, the Mexican office designed to assist migrants, was crying. She said, "Dora, this is horrible. We've never seen this. We don't know how to help these people. They don't speak Spanish. They are lost and scared. They have come from thousands of miles away, and their smugglers are no longer answering their calls."

It was as if the smugglers and U.S. Border Patrol were playing ping-pong, but with people seeking asylum. Migrants were being guided across the border into the U.S. by their smugglers, only to be expelled shortly after. Often without a chance to properly request asylum.

This was especially common during the Title 42 policy, which allowed rapid expulsions under public health grounds. It created a terrible situation for people desperately seeking safety. Despite the risks, many continued to follow the advice of smugglers and cartels. The cartels profited enormously and had a strong incentive to convince migrants they would be welcomed into the U.S., not expelled.

When the Biden Administration took office, it introduced a new process for requesting asylum appointments through a mobile application called CBP One (U.S. Customs and Border Protection One). While not the only way to seek asylum, it quickly became the primary method at official ports of entry. The administration claimed it would reduce unauthorized crossings, but in practice, it forced many asylum seekers to wait in dangerous Mexican border towns.

Many of these individuals didn't have smartphones or access to the technology required to use the app. These areas were often perilous, and the new system left the most vulnerable even more exposed to cartel violence and exploitation.

We learned that smugglers and cartels communicated with each other and with migrants via WhatsApp. Many people making the journey would receive the same message: "Come to the wall and present yourself. Ignore what else you've heard. This is the correct method, and you will be allowed into the U.S." These messages created false hope. When people reached the port of entry, they were met with a reality that was anything but predictable. The system was wildly inconsistent.

For example, among ten men from Africa, two might be allowed to stay in the U.S. while the other eight are deported to Mexico. Those two allowed to stay might send home messages saying, "Yes, it works like they said," reinforcing a cycle of misleading information and hope based on incomplete or lucky outcomes. Ultimately, it's the people who pay the price. Waiting and hoping, caught in a system that sees their desperation but rarely their humanity. And still, they keep coming.

Chapter Sixteen

Threads of Hope

Alongside Salvavision's volunteers, the local women of Sasabe, who now operate Casa de la Esperanza, continued to meet migrants with immediate aid: food, water, a place to rest, and perhaps most importantly, human dignity. But it was not always this way.

When we first met, the small group of women who would become the center's backbone did not view the migrants in the same way I did. To them, these were just people passing through, a steady stream of strangers moving across their town.

At first, the increase in arrivals was overwhelming. The change in the town's daily life was hard to ignore. We heard sentiments like, "They are sleeping on our porches," "They are filling the plaza, it is always packed," and "They are taking over the town."

I hoped to lead by example in how we treated our guests respectfully, and we insisted on calling everyone by their first names. A phrase I often used with volunteers and staff was, "They are people just like you and me." Over time, the local women began to see their impact as they greeted people with care and kindness.

One of the first ways we built a connection was by starting an embroidery collective, where women from the community gathered every Wednesday afternoon to embroider cloth tote bags, drink coffee, and talk. The bags were sold on Salvavision's website and at events, with the money going directly to the women. They were getting paid for their work, for their art. This was real work, something they were creating and bringing to life.

It was a completely different narrative from what the cartels offered. The cartels offered quick money, but those recruited were expendable. They were killed, and someone else would take their place, believing they could do it better, that they would survive.

As we became closer to the women in the embroidery program, they began to share their stories. We learned that they had been alone and isolated before the center opened. They sat in their homes watching TV, losing their sense of community. They had no one to talk to about the pandemic, how things were changing, and the many ways they all needed support. But as they came together, something started to change.

We watched the transformation as they came together and began to trust each other. We would walk into the center full of women looking down at the tote bag they were working on, laughing and carrying on like teenagers. It felt like a middle school slumber party.

They started to open up, sharing funny moments with their kids, venting about their husbands, and confiding in one another about experiences of domestic violence. In some cases, abusers were held accountable. The women began to protect each other. They offered support, shared ideas, and built something that felt like family.

Some told us they had started saving money. One woman bought a car. Another, a young woman paralyzed from the waist down, could buy a wheelchair. Before that, her mother carried her into the center so that she could join the embroidery group. Her work was stunning, and she took immense pride in it. The first time I saw her arrive unassisted in her new wheelchair, I cried. Her father later built a ramp so she could enter on her own. Everyone contributed to and benefited from the many gifts of Casa de la Esperanza.

As the program expanded, it also reached a village in Guatemala, where thirteen women gathered to embroider their beautiful *mantas* and connect with one another. Even though they might only earn $40 to $80 a month, it makes a real difference in their lives and the lives of their families. They love the craft that has been passed down for generations and take pride in their work. The money is deeply appreciated.

Over the past three years since the opening of the center, the women in the Sasabe embroidery collective began to see migrants in a new light. Living in a border town, they were used to seeing people pass through, but they had never had the chance to hear their stories or offer help. I proposed that they each volunteer one weekend day per month at the center. They started signing up, and before long, they were showing up with open hearts, offering Tylenol, helping someone find the shower, or serving meals. Everyone's life was changed.

The number of people heading north kept rising, including more and more unaccompanied minors, some as young as seven. One day, a group of children arrived at our door, asking for help. It broke my heart. As humanitarian aid workers, we were not allowed to touch these children, even when we suspected they were being trafficked. I reminded myself that many parents paid someone to guide their kids north, hoping they would be safer that way.

We never know the full story of the person standing before us. But what I have learned over the years is this: the most powerful thing we can offer is simple kindness, a warm meal, a safe shower, a place to rest. Those small acts stay with you. They change the way you see everything.

And that's the kind of care we built Casa de la Esperanza on. The work there went far beyond meeting basic needs. A U.S.-based group, *Veterans for Peace*, adopted the center and built two big playgrounds where local children could finally play. Before that, they had nowhere to go. I had long feared that the cartels might begin targeting young kids for recruitment. I hoped that these safe, welcoming spaces would give them another path.

Other groups helped too, painting murals and creating beauty where there had been none. Gail suggested outdoor movie nights, with films projected on the side of the building. The town needed more things for its young people. Local teachers began using the center in the evenings to work on lesson plans. We had Wi-Fi and air conditioning, though no furnace for the cold winter nights.

We also started a small Spanish-language library, open to both migrants and the local community. It quickly became a lifeline. One of our next projects was to build a memorial park to honor those who had died in the desert. Even the saguaros that surrounded us, once forgotten, began to receive care. With help from Salvavision, we paid someone to water them. No detail was too small. Every act of care mattered.

Sometimes, locals would bring people to us who had been injured in the desert, migrants who hadn't even reached the U.S. border yet. They knew the center was a place where everyone would be treated with dignity.

Part of our mission was also to prevent forced migration when we could. We understand that people have to flee danger, but when poverty is the reason, and that poverty can be addressed, many would rather stay home, especially mothers forced to leave their children, or kids making the journey alone.

I'll never forget one snowy night when Gail, working on the U.S. side of the border, found a Salvadoran brother and sister with no food or shelter. She immediately called me to translate over the phone, while they were waiting for Border Patrol, hoping to request asylum. When the agents arrived, the siblings were taken into custody and later deported to Nogales, Mexico.

Eventually, the brother lost hope and decided to cross again, but this time on his own. He was caught and deported back to El Salvador. When I spoke to him after he arrived home, I asked if he was glad to be back. He said yes. Things weren't much safer, but they had improved since he left, and he was reunited with his young son. Salvavision helped pay for his barber training, and later, I saw him again, living and working in the very town where I grew up. He was happy. He had never wanted to leave, only felt he had no choice.

As for the sister, she moved to Mexico City and started a new life there. Though they went their separate ways, they both found new beginnings after a long, difficult journey.

On another trip to El Salvador, I met a young mother with a four-year-old daughter. She had just returned from Mexico after trying to reach the U.S. and was barely getting by. There was a sadness in her eyes I won't forget. We connected instantly, like mother and daughter. I told her Salvavision would support her education.

Four years later, she's nearly finished with her social work degree. We've helped with tuition, food, rent, whatever she needed. Today, she works in immigration services, helping others who have returned to their home country. Her story, like so many, has come full circle. And seeing that gives me hope.

Looking back, this journey has shown me what's possible when we come together, when communities, organizations, and individuals join hands. We can't do it alone. We're not meant to.

I think of all we built in Sasabe, the faces, the stories, the solidarity. It wasn't just the women in the embroidery collective or the migrants who passed through. It was everyone who believed that, together, we could make a difference.

However, while we worked to build a foundation of care and dignity, the world outside continued to shift. The crisis didn't stop at our doors. It reached far into the desert, into places where survival meant more than food or shelter.

Chapter Seventeen

What Remains
Organ Pipe Cactus National Monument
Arizona, Spring 2024

"I survived the tragedy, but thirteen others did not,
including an unborn child."

I don't want to pull these students away from the moment. I can sense they are beginning to understand, starting to feel the weight of what it takes to leave everything behind and step into the unknown. I want them to connect, not just intellectually, but with their hearts to the families, the mothers, fathers, and children who risk everything.

I've walked in those shoes. I know that fear. I know what it feels like to be completely alone and afraid no one will ever find you.

They're listening now. The students from Northwestern stand completely still.

"After we were rescued, we spent several days in the hospital in Ajo. Then I was taken to jail in Tucson for a couple of nights. None of us had family in Tucson, and almost everyone was heading to Los Angeles or different parts of the country," I continued.

"The authorities were going to prosecute the smugglers for human trafficking. We would be the state's main evidence. Asylum was never mentioned." I pause. I want the students to understand this. "If there had not been this trial, we would have been sent back immediately. The only reason we could stay was because we were material witnesses to the crime, and punishing the smugglers was more important than keeping us out of the country."

Around us, thirteen bright crosses dot the desert ground, symbolic graves that mark the site of that tragedy. I scan the students' faces. Troubled. Thoughtful. I decided to shift the focus.

"My faith gives me resiliency. I hope your faith helps you, too." Slight smiles and nods.

"We go through so much, especially women. It's hard to give back when you think you have nothing left. But you'll be amazed by how much you can give once you realize that giving can heal you. That's been my salvation."

I turned to the pastor. "Would you like to offer a prayer?"

He looks at his students. "How about we sing a song?"

Three boys lean in toward each other and begin singing in Latin. I hear Sister Judy's voice join them. *Salve Regina. Hail, Holy Queen.* I imagine the spirits of those lost listening as this song floats into the clear blue sky.

"You sound like angels," I say. "Angels in the desert."

I brought flowers. Three pink carnations for the sisters, and a yellow lily for the unborn child. I kneel by the small blue cross in front of the taller white one. My gaze lingers. The official record says thirteen died, but I know the truth. There were fourteen souls lost.

I have since learned the sisters' names: Alicia, Inés, and Juanita. They were buried decades ago in Los Angeles.

I tell the students, "You can say whatever prayer you want as you place your flowers at whatever cross you choose."

They move among the crosses, kneeling, whispering, and gently fixing rosaries that have become tangled by the wind.

Some sit apart, quiet and thoughtful.

As we neared the trucks, I let the students walk ahead of me. Their voices were hushed now, their footsteps soft against the desert ground. The crosses behind us. I paused, turning once more to look back.

I thought of Casa de la Esperanza, the painted walls, the laughter, the quiet strength of the women who built it with me, brick by brick, prayer by prayer. I had wanted to take these students there. To show them where hope once lived out loud. But I couldn't. Not anymore.

I turned to the students. "We live in a protected world," I said. "I don't want to scare you. But you need to understand how different it is when you don't have the privileges we take for granted in the United States."

"In Mexico and other countries, you are not safe to speak out. I would have loved to take you to see Casa de la Esperanza, in Sasabe, Sonora, but we've had to close it. The immigration system has created wars along the border, for control, for profit. Smuggling people is now more lucrative than smuggling drugs."

I don't want to say more, afraid I might lose composure in front of these young people. My grief sits heavy in my chest. I thought our beautiful center would continue to thrive and expand over the years. We poured our hearts into it. And now it's gone.

A cartel war took it all. We're waiting to see what remains, and whether we will ever be allowed to return. The thought of rebuilding from scratch is more than daunting. It feels impossible. Casa de la Esperanza was our home. Our prayer. Our rebellion. Our hope. And now, it is only a memory. I don't know if I have it in me to begin again.

We're still waiting to see how the dust settles. Which cartel will take control? Will they let us come back? Will there even be a building left standing? Would it be safe to try?

The thought of rebuilding, re-earning trust, of starting from zero again is almost too much to carry. Casa de la Esperanza was never just a place. It was our baby. A home built with love and sweat and sisterhood. And now, it's gone. Not just a financial loss. A loss of family. A loss of what we dreamed together.

Maybe it will return. Maybe someone else will take up the vision. But I don't think it will be me. I will still show up in other ways and do the work that calls me. But I won't know this new community.

A student's voice pulls me back, "What about the migrants we saw yesterday? Were they going to apply for asylum?"

One of the chaperones answers first, explaining the CBP One app, which serves as a digital gatekeeper, and how people must submit their information, wait for a response, wait for a date, and then wait for permission to request safety.

Another student asks, "But what if they're already in Sonoyta, Mexico? How long do they wait?"

I know the answer. Months. Maybe longer. They sleep in tents. On sidewalks. In makeshift camps where danger lurks in the shadows. They are hunted. Kidnapped. Held for ransom. Their lives reduced to waiting for a phone notification, for a miracle, for someone to see them.

We climb back into the trucks. No one speaks. The sun hangs low, and behind us, the crosses still stand.

Chapter Eighteen

A Community Unraveled
Sasabe, Sonora, Mexico, October 2023

It wasn't just the memory of Casa de la Esperanza that weighed on me. While I mourned its closing, violence escalated in Sasabe in ways none of us had ever imagined.

Rosa, a resident of Sasabe, called me on a Sunday. Her voice trembled with fear as she told me there was fighting in the town. She and the other residents were terrified. A new cartel had arrived, determined to take control. Gunfire echoed through the streets, and houses were being burned to the ground.

People in the village anxiously waited for the Mexican government to step in and protect them, especially since the violence was so close to the United States border, but help never came. They were caught in an absolute nightmare within their community.

People were trapped. They couldn't flee south, deeper into Mexico, because cartels controlled that area, kidnapping people and burning cars. They couldn't go north past the port of entry in Sasabe, Arizona, as they were repeatedly denied entry into the United States, despite the fundamental human right to seek asylum protected by the Universal Declaration of Human Rights.

One young man was shot three times, right in town. Since there are no medical facilities in Sasabe, he was rushed to the port of entry, but turned away by United States agents. He was denied emergency medical assistance and died an hour later.

Families who made it to the U.S. spent days in immigration centers, separated and full of fear. Some were reunited with family, others detained, and some were deported back into the violence they'd fled. Children were taken from their parents, like a one-month-old baby whose mother forgot her birth certificate in her rush to escape the war zone.

The town's population shrank from 2,500 to about 30 families. Many sought refuge east to Nogales or west to Sonoyta. Others were granted entry through different ports. I scrambled to find temporary housing for those granted Humanitarian Parole, and with the help of partner organizations, we found housing for most of them.

Amid this chaos, I was in contact with a father from Sasabe whose oldest son was murdered when the war between the cartel gangs began. Desperate to protect his other son, who had been receiving death threats, he sought my help to get him out of the town.

I went to the port of entry in Sasabe, Arizona, with the son's wife and their two small children, who had been living with a support family in Tucson. I shared their story, but the port of entry staff turned the father away, sending him back into Mexico and back into extreme danger.

I saw the deep sadness in his children's eyes as the Customs Agent told them, "You can hug your dad, but he has to go back to Sasabe." In moments like these, my heart feels as though it might burst from my chest as I witness the utter lack of compassion shown to so many. This was one of those moments. And this was when I knew I had to become a vocal advocate for this man. I reminded myself not to be afraid to speak up, even if I was pint-sized compared to the tall, strong agent standing between this father and his freedom.

The Customs Agent listened as I explained why I do this work of love. After what felt like an eternity, he said, "Okay, call me at five p.m." So, I did, and he replied, "Have the man show up at nine a.m. tomorrow. I'll see what I can do." The next morning, after waiting six hours with his wife and children at the port of entry, we left with the father for Tucson.

Experiences like this, helping this man whose life was at risk and who was finally able to cross the border legally into the United States, keep me going in this work. Like many in the humanitarian aid sector, I often feel frustrated with the system. The political rhetoric wears me down, and I grow disheartened by how politicians exploit human suffering to further their agendas.

In quieter moments, I reflect on my tragedy that occurred over forty years ago. Things seem the same, or worse. The cruelty intensifies, people are treated more inhumanely, and hate is more visible. These thoughts bring loneliness, anger, and fear. But I return to the truth of who I am and why I chose this path. I've always worked to see the good in others. I've dedicated my life to advocating for those who can't speak for themselves. None of that has changed.

I know there is still good in the world, and I refuse to let the darkness take me down.

So, I remind myself: *Okay, Dora, you're not alone.* There are many of us fighting for the same cause, saving lives and reuniting families. I'm part of a whole network of people doing this work together.

I hold close the love and support of my friends and family. I feel it in the words they say, in the ways they show up, and in the quiet strength they offer when things feel overwhelming. I met Sister Judy during visits to detention centers, and she's become a dear friend. A nun and retired social worker, she lives simply and serves with deep compassion. She makes me laugh, challenges me, and reminds me what it means to love boldly.

Others have come into my life through this work, such as

Bob Kee, who is steady and kind, and Francisco Cantú, a former Border Patrol agent whose book, The Line Becomes a River, wrestles with many of the same questions we carry. The friendships I've made over the years are too many to count, but they all share one thing: each person is committed to bringing dignity and safety to those in search of a better life.

People often ask, "How can you keep doing this after everything you've been through?" I answer, "That's where my strength comes from. I lived it. I know the fear. I know the terror. While I may not know exactly what they're feeling, I've walked a similar path, and I care deeply."

I see and hear the stories of the desert in a way others might not. I see the pain in the eyes of those who, like I once did, carry the weight of their struggles. I want to tell them, "I know. I've been there. I've done it too." I want them to know that I understand why they are doing this. I remember the mix of excitement and fear I felt knowing I was going to the United States, packing fast and only bringing the things that mattered most to me: a Bible from my mother, a picture of my family, some food, all carried through the desert in my little backpack.

I think about that father at the port of entry, holding his children, scared and lost. I think of all the others who have been turned away and forced back into danger. I remember how I felt when I was in their shoes. I know what it's like to be afraid and desperate. That's what connects me to them.

When the darkness feels too heavy, I remind myself that I am not alone. And as long as we have each other, I will keep going. Every day presents an opportunity to make a difference. And that's enough for me.

Chapter Nineteen

Organ Pipe Cactus
National Monument, Arizona, Spring 2024

The sun is starting to set as we pull into the gravel lot where we first met. My mind is still heavy with everything that's happening just beyond the border in Sasabe, the stories that linger, the ones that weigh on me. But now, I shift my focus back to the students beside me. It's time to debrief.

Before I agreed to bring them to the site where I was rescued, I took the time to learn about the Sheil Catholic Center. Their mission is to witness love through vibrant worship, transformative learning, and prophetic justice. I've tried to keep that in mind as I've shared what I could with the students, being honest about the truth but not too overwhelming. I want them to understand without closing themselves off to the pain of others. The road ahead for those choosing humanitarian aid will be a tough one, I know. It's one thing to witness the tragedy. It's another to feel the weight of it day after day.

But I also want them to know there are victories. The kind of victories that never make the headlines, but make all the difference.

My life didn't stop because of what happened out here," I say, looking at their faces. "It pushed me to show up for others. We see so many people at the wall, in the desert, in the shelters. And most of the time, we don't know what happens to them after that. But sometimes, I'm lucky enough to stay connected. I get phone calls around the holidays, around Mother's Day. They reach out just to connect and thank me. It means everything."

I pull out my phone and scroll through my photos until I find Leyda's smiling face. There she is, her four children beside her, all smiles now in Texas. I had previously told them about a journalist from *Human Rights Watch* who had contacted me regarding Leyda's family. She had interviewed me a while back and kept my number for times when people like Leyda needed help, and no one else knew where to turn.

She had called me about a mother and her four children, who were stuck in Monterrey, Mexico. "They're from Honduras," she'd said. "She's living on the streets, no food, nothing for the kids. She's terrified of the people who threatened her back home. She's sure they're still following her."

I can see that the students are leaning in now, their attention fully captured. They want to know how I could possibly help someone so far away, in such desperate need.

"Well, I talked to Sister Lika, the Director of *La Casa de la Misericordia* in Nogales, Sonora," I continued. "She told me they'd have space for them if they could make it there. Sister Lika's shelter is a lifeline for so many families waiting for their asylum process to be completed. It's a place of safety and care when so many other shelters can't offer that kind of support."

"I told the journalist I'd send money for bus tickets to Nogales. I made sure Leyda knew that if she didn't feel too unsafe going to the bus station, she could take the bus and head there. Sister Lika was expecting them."

One of the students raises her hand. "How did you send money to Mexico?" I smile. "I used to use Western Union, but they kept cutting me off, thinking I was doing something shady because I sent so much to the border. It was frustrating,"

I laugh, though it's more out of disbelief than amusement. "But then a migrant told me about WorldRemit. It's easier, cheaper, and they never cut me off."

The students are still listening, absorbing. "They made it to Nogales," I say, "and eventually, they immigrated legally into the U.S."

I share another story of success, this one from the time I visited Casa San Pedro, a shelter in Sonoyta, Sonora. "It was there that I helped my first Salvadoran family, a mother, father, and three children. I didn't know what I could do at first, but we managed to get them across legally simply by guiding them and explaining their rights. It was a victory that felt like the world had tilted in the right direction."

I tell the students how we advised the family to find someone they trusted to drive them to the port of entry in Lukeville, Arizona. It wasn't a regular port, as they only processed one family a day, but they went anyway, hoping to be chosen.

One day, I got the call. The mother's voice on the other end, *"Dorita, estamos aquí."* The immigration officials needed my information, so I sent over a copy of my driver's license. I had arranged for a sponsor family in Tucson, since I didn't have room in my own house. A lovely family with a beautiful home and pool said they'd pick them up.

But then, the unexpected happened. Four hours later, I learned the family was being sent to Phoenix, not Tucson. CBP had changed its processing center. I called the sponsor family, and they said, "Just send us the new address, we'll go get them."

"Oh my God," I say to the students, a grin on my face. "By 5 p.m., the kids were swimming in that couple's pool. They had never seen a pool before."

Later, another volunteer from the Tucson Samaritans offered

them a space after they left their first sponsor's home. They stayed there for six months before moving to Houston with another family.

"They're doing great," I tell the students. "They're still in the asylum process. Their case probably won't be heard for ten years, but they now have work permits. The children are thriving. I get pictures of them from time to time. They're a happy family. They've flourished because they were given a chance."

I look at the students, hoping this moment stays with them, hoping they leave here wanting to learn more, to dig deeper into what's happening on the border. I want them to know that their help, no matter how small, matters.

"I have my story to share," I say softly. "But I see young people like you doing good work out there, at the wall, leaving water for those who need it. Every one of you has something to share. Something that opened your eyes, something that changed you. It's that first spark that sends you down this path of humanitarian aid."

Just then, James steps away to one of the trucks. I take this as an opportunity to tell the students about his work while he's out of earshot, wanting them to fully understand the importance of his work.

"James Holeman," I point to him, "arranged for another driver today and got both trucks ready for this difficult drive." I pause to give the students a moment to watch him. James is busy arranging vehicle recovery items in the bed of the pickup: traction boards, a heavy high-lift jack, a six-foot-long pry bar, a tow strap and shackle, a shovel, and also cases of bottled water, electrolyte drinks, and a basket of energy bars. I know he leaves these on his trucks during searches, in case migrants come by needing food and water.

"He's a Marine Corps veteran who started a group called

Battalion Search and Rescue. He leads self-trained volunteers into the remote reaches of the borderland desert, searching for migrants who are distressed or deceased. The Battalion is in a race against time. The Sonoran Desert is brutal, and it quickly erases any trace of human life. The sooner they're found, the better the chance for identification, family reunification, and a proper burial. His group, along with others like it, provides families with the opportunity for closure. Not knowing what happened to someone you love can be more painful than knowing they're gone."

I watch the students as they observe James moving the recovery items around in the truck. It's another chance to plant a seed about how people can serve and make a difference. I decided to share one more example of people helping people.

"There are endless ways to help," I say. "A volunteer from Witness at the Border, whom I've never met, sent me hand warmers to distribute to asylum seekers in Sasabe during the colder months. I made sure to send her a photo of a young child receiving one, and the donor turned around and sent me a box of individual applesauce packets. These might seem like small gestures, but they have an incredible impact on people on these terrible journeys."

Help always shows up. It's how I survive the chaos. I never know where the donations will come from, but they always do. When Salvavision is down or struggling, I take a deep breath. A check will arrive, two hundred or three hundred dollars, right when I need it.

"There's never a donation too big or too small," I say. "Whatever it is, it's always enough."

We are a small organization, but the work we do matters.

As I wrap up, I turn to the group and say, "We are on a journey together in solidarity. We, as a collective, are working alongside others and within our communities. We don't solve all their problems, but we are there in the moment, offering what's needed. We remind people that they matter, that there are kind people in the world who care."

I add, "I hope that when you return home, you can give people a firsthand account of what things are really like here, show them a different side of what they're hearing in the news."

Before I can finish, a young man pipes up, his voice eager "Oh, we will."

His quick response makes me laugh. It's moments like this that remind me how powerful it is when people carry these stories home, passing them on and keeping them alive.

"One last story before we say goodbye," I say, then laugh along with the students. "Okay, perhaps now you can see how my desire to help could have gotten me in trouble in my volatile country. I have always wanted to make things better. If I see a fire, I have to put it out. If there's a crisis, I have to deal with it. I try to find solutions. That's how I am, how my brain works. I don't always find the right solutions, and that's okay. I'm open to criticism. I don't know it all that's for sure, but I have always said the only way we can make this better is together. Come along with me and we'll do it together."

I take a breath and bring it around full circle again.

"When I was at the wall a few weeks ago, I met a young child, an unaccompanied minor who had traveled up from Guatemala without any family members, only strangers. For me, he embodied the story of migration. I have read countless books on the borderlands, on refugees, migrants, asylum seekers, and immigration. Every time I read a new story, it brings me hope because in it, there is courage and resilience. It shows that we move forward with the hope of what can be. The most important lesson I've taken from all of these books is how people who come to the United States trust this country and love this country."

I stop and breathe.

"And here was this little boy in front of me, hopeful, excited. He is currently in the United States. He had made it."

"Where are you going, Kevin?" I asked.

"To my aunt's house," he said.

He wriggled at the waist, then turned slightly so I could see. Inked inside the waistband of his pants was an address, handwritten and beginning to fade. He looked up at me and smiled, a little shy but full of hope. At that moment, I saw more than a boy with a destination. I saw myself, a younger me, just as full of hope. I remembered traveling to this "land of opportunity" with my aunt and uncle's address tucked into a tiny pocket my mother had sewn into my underwear. Her quiet way of keeping me safe. Her way of sending me off with something to hold onto.

"What happened to the little boy?" a student asks.

"Who knows?" I say, pausing.

"That's the nature of this work. We show up. We do our best. We try to help, making things a little easier and kinder. And then we let go, not because we don't care, but because we have to. We carry them with us, but we move on."

With that, the long day finally winds down. The students begin gathering their belongings. I watch them leave, wondering what they'll take with them, what will stay in their hearts, long after they've gone back to their lives.

In some ways, I feel that same question about the survivors of my own story: Where are they now? What have they become? How have they carried the weight of what we went through?

Chapter Twenty

I Carry On for Them

Some stories don't have clear endings. They live on in the people who survive, in the ones left behind, and in our memories. I think often about those who crossed the desert with me. Not just about what happened to us back then, but how those moments shaped the rest of our lives. We each walked away from that tragedy in different directions. I've often wished I could reconnect with more of them, to see if any have become humanitarians like the friends I work alongside today.

My cousin Ricardo was seventeen when we crossed. Now in his late fifties, he still carries the weight of that experience. He doesn't talk about it. I once said to him, "Come with me. Let's do this work together. People still need help." But he couldn't. It's something he's kept buried.

My Uncle Carlos also survived the journey. He built a life here as a truck driver, moving goods across the country. Years later, he was diagnosed with AIDS. When his health declined, I brought him from California to Tucson to care for him. He spent his last four years between the hospital and a nursing home. He passed away in his early fifties, too young. But he lived with strength and resilience, right to the end.

I've stayed connected with another survivor, José, who now lives here in Tucson. He's always been quiet and doesn't talk much about the tragedy. But during the journey, it was his guitar that often lifted our spirits when everything around us felt so heavy. Now, in his mid-eighties, he has built a family and a life of his own.

We all carry it differently. Some of us talk about it. Some of us don't. But we're all still living with it in our own way.

I once received a phone call from a young woman living in California. Her father was Don Cruz, the religious man who was always holding and reading from his Bible. This call came forty years after our crossing. She had been only seven when her father left, and had never seen him again. She wanted to know how he had died.

"Come out, *hija*. We'll go to the site together and pay our respects," I said. "We'll offer prayers for him."

She went quiet. Maybe it was too painful to talk about. She told me she was one of six children. Their mother had died still waiting for him to come home. She never accepted that he was gone. His body never made it back to El Salvador. They didn't have the money. He's buried in Tucson, with the others. His daughter has never made the trip here.

Not long after, I got a call from a relative of Felícita, the frail young woman who died in her aunt's arms in the desert. She told me her father had been looking for someone to talk to. Felícita had been his little sister.

When I visited El Salvador, I met with him. He cried, deeply, like a child who had been holding it in for too long. He told me their relationship had been complicated. He believed that if he had been kinder to her, maybe she wouldn't have left. He never got the chance to say goodbye. In his heart, he felt like he had pushed her into that journey. The guilt stayed with him. Heavy and raw.

I have deep compassion for those who leave home, because no matter the reason, you are never the same. Even without tragedy, stepping onto someone else's land makes you a guest.

You've left behind the people who loved you most - your

family, your mother, your father. Imagine not knowing if you'll ever see your mother again.

Leaving my country and my family was the hardest part for me. I never imagined it. And even now, years later, I still feel like I don't fully belong here. This is my second home. This is my second language. I don't speak perfect English. I have an accent. I make up words that don't always make sense. But I know I'm doing something important. I know I'm affecting lives, not only the lives of those seeking safety, but also the lives of those who work alongside me.

I received a text recently from a fellow volunteer. He was from *No More Deaths* and had been providing EMT services to asylum seekers. "Hello, Dora. This is Eric. We met yesterday. Just wanted to say it was an honor to meet you. You're an energy of the desert that I draw inspiration from. Meeting you for just ten minutes stirred emotions I've kept hidden and made me a slightly wiser human. Thank you."

Where will these young people from Northwestern University end up? What kind of work will they do? Maybe some will be like Eric the EMT, giving direct aid at the border. Maybe they'll be the ones who give a packet of crackers to a mother from Africa and her child, who haven't eaten for fourteen hours. Maybe they'll offer a smile, a hug, a welcome—letting someone know they're glad they made it, glad they're here.

That kindness, those small actions, they mean so much.

Resettlement is never easy for asylum seekers. They pass through immigration centers, facing background checks, long interviews, and endless waiting. Even a small issue can land them in detention or a federal facility, adding another layer of hardship.

I often think how much more they could offer if we gave them work permits sooner, they could contribute, pay taxes, fill jobs that need hands and hearts. They don't want to hide or work in the shadows. They want a chance to belong, to build a life with dignity. And too often, we make them prove their worth again and again, even after they've already survived some of life's hardest trials.

The system is flawed, no question. But still, I see people kissing the ground when they cross into the U.S. I see others at the border, walking around in a daze, clutching crumpled papers with their asylum dates written on them. The numbers stretch into the thousands. Where are they supposed to go while they wait?

This journey—my journey, has been one of tragedy, resilience, hope, and humanity. And as I look back, I understand that this is not just my story. It's the story of all of us—struggling, surviving, and showing up in solidarity.

The work isn't over. We have to keep showing up, keep fighting for what's right, and keep giving hope, even when it feels like there's none left. It's not enough to just witness. We must act. We must stand together.

It is through this work that I heal. It is through this work that we all heal.

And it is through showing up, again and again, that we build the future we all deserve.

Afterword

I have always wanted this book to become my legacy, something I could leave in writing for future generations, for my children and grandchildren. I also hope it serves as an educational tool in schools, a resource to help others understand how the United States has been involved in shaping the political and economic landscapes of other countries. This involvement has often contributed to instability, upheaval, and the forced migration of entire communities.

This story illustrates what happens when people are forced to flee their homes, not by choice, but out of necessity, when the decision to leave becomes a matter of life or death, sometimes made in days, sometimes in moments.

My history encompasses the most crucial moments of immigration. It is shocking how few people know about the role the United States played in the wars of Central America, conflicts that continue to drive migration to this day. We are still feeling those repercussions.

I also wanted to show how someone can live through trauma, as I have, and still come out the other side determined to do good in the world. There are countless stories like mine: stories of survival after sexual assault, domestic violence, and unimaginable hardship. I wanted to add my voice, and the voices of those who shared my journey in the desert, to the growing chorus of people who are not just surviving, but creating change. I survived, and I've become a part of a movement that saves lives. It is an incredible, full-circle experience.

This story also affirms the importance of asylum. It reveals the heart of most people crossing our border, and what becomes possible when someone is simply given another chance.

Throughout my experiences, I have never witnessed an "invasion" at our southern borders. What I have seen over and over again is an opportunity. An opportunity to welcome children, women, men, and all people who are placing their trust in this country, hoping for protection and the chance at a better life.

I imagine a world where every person is treated with dignity, respect, and kindness, regardless of their skin color, gender identity, or place of birth. We all live under one sky.

Dora Rodriguez

Acknowledgments

Thank you, Alvaro Enciso, thank you from the bottom of my heart. After 35 years of searching, it was you who allowed me to find the place where 13 of my friends died and where 13 of us were rescued. Thank you for your mission to honor each person who dies in our Arizona Desert, a place we knew as where dreams died, until worse was revealed. I am forever thankful to be able to visit this holy site, say a prayer, and find some peace. I can only hope the same for the other families and their loved ones who have visited this site since, and for the spirits who rest there.

To my children, Eric, Javier, Cynthia, Trever, and Anna—you are each the reason for my existence. I'm a proud mother, and now a grandmother, Abuelita. May you carry forward lives rooted in justice, peace, and solidarity toward a better world. I love you all deeply.

To my dear son Trever—I will always hold close to my heart the moments we spent talking about the design of this book. You were so gentle, so thoughtful, carefully going through old photos of me, and turning them into something beautiful. I am honored and proud to have your work as the cover and back cover of my story, a story of resilience, hope, and resistance.

To David—thank you for your unconditional love, and for showing me that it is never too late to find your soulmate. I love you dearly.

To my sweet mother—thank you for watching over me every day. I miss you more than words can say.

To my siblings, Mary, Meme, and Oscar—although I had to leave when you were all still so young, and we didn't get to grow old together, the love and gratitude we share continues to give me strength.

And to Gail, Blanquita, Almita, and Ofelia—thank you for your love, compassion, and kindness toward our guests at Casa de la Esperanza. Your spirit and open hearts made our work possible.

Call to Action

Volunteer some of your free time and take the opportunity to learn the real stories of our borderlands, of the people fleeing their countries because of climate change, violence, poverty, gender persecution, religious oppression, or political beliefs. Get involved with your local community, and don't be afraid to show up. Always seek out your passion and your interests, and continue to find community with others who share your values. Above all, spread love and kindness wherever you go.

Groups to Get Involved With

Ajo Samaritans

Ajo Samaritans continue the historical work of providing water and other humanitarian aid to travelers in the desert in the Ajo, Arizona area, regardless of their immigration status. We also engage with our community and collaborative groups to raise awareness of the systemic causes of death and suffering of travelers near the U.S./Mexico border and to provide access to humanitarian resources.

Battalion Search and Rescue

The Battalion Search and Rescue is an Arizona- and New Mexico-based search and rescue organization focusing on lost and missing migrants. We are a self-trained, community-based group that reaches remote areas of the Arizona and New Mexico deserts every month. Our volunteers come from a wide range of backgrounds but have the same mission: to save lives and provide closure for families and loved ones.

The Border Chronicle

The Border Chronicle is a weekly newsletter that publishes original, on-the-ground reporting, analysis, and commentary. Every Tuesday and Thursday, subscribers will receive our latest dispatch in their inbox. We also host a podcast where we talk to fascinating fronterizos, artists, activists, asylum seekers, and others. Our goal is to challenge preconceived notions about the borderlands, even our own. We want to create a community of ideas so we can break free of the "crisis" narrative that does such a disservice to our region.

Border Community Alliance

Border Community Alliance is bridging the border and fostering community through education, collaboration, and cultural exchange. We focus on accomplishing this pursuit in the borderlands region of Southern Arizona/Sonora, Mexico. We are inspired to share with the public the good news of civil society in the international borderlands region.

BorderLinks

BorderLinks is a community-based organization where people collectively learn, teach, reflect, share resources, and organize for justice in the borderlands. Through popular education rooted in place and lived experience, BorderLinks and community partners inspire and ignite action to transform unjust borders and (im)migration laws and conditions. We belong to movements for social transformation and collective liberation.

Casa de la Misericordia y de Todas las Naciones

Casa de la Misericordia is a migrant shelter in Nogales, Sonora, Mexico.

Catholic Community Services of Southern Arizona

Clients, staff, volunteers, donors . . . We're from many backgrounds and many walks of life, but we are all part of the Catholic Community Services of Southern Arizona family. Together, our work touches lives every day, in great and small ways. While our services are many, one thread binds our work together: We help children, families, and individuals live with independence and dignity.

Florence Project

The Florence Project's mission is to provide free legal and social services to detained adults and unaccompanied children facing immigration removal proceedings in Arizona.

Green Valley-Sahuarita Samaritans

The mission of Samaritans is to save lives and relieve suffering in the Arizona borderlands...We are compassionate individuals committed to saving lives in the southern Arizona desert. We believe in respect for human rights and one's ethical responsibility to assist those who are suffering.

Hope Border Institute

The Hope Border Institute (HOPE) brings the perspective of Catholic social teaching to bear on the realities unique to our U.S.-Mexico border region. Through a robust program of research and policy work, leadership development, and action, we work to build justice and deepen solidarity across the borderlands.

Human Rights Watch

Human Rights Watch investigates and reports on abuses happening in all corners of the world. We are roughly 550-plus people of 70-plus nationalities who are country experts, lawyers, journalists, and others who work to protect the most at-risk, from vulnerable minorities and civilians in wartime, to refugees and children in need. We direct our advocacy toward governments, armed groups, and businesses, pushing them to change or enforce their laws, policies, and practices. To ensure our independence, we refuse government funding and carefully review all donations to ensure that they are consistent with our policies, mission, and values. We partner with organizations large and small across the globe to protect embattled activists and to help hold abusers to account and bring justice to victims.

Humane Borders

Humane Borders, motivated by faith and the universal need for kindness, established a system of water stations in the Sonoran Desert on routes used by migrants making the perilous journey here on foot. Our primary mission is to save desperate people from a horrible death by dehydration and exposure. Creating a just and humane environment in the borderlands is vital to this mission. To that end, we work with government land managers and nonprofit groups to make water and other lifesaving resources available to migrants on both sides of the border.

Founded in the summer of 2000, Humane Borders, Inc. is a nonprofit corporation that, since its beginning, has worked in the desert with the support of hundreds of volunteers, Pima County, and the City of Tucson. Volunteering is our primary way of educating the public about how they can help diminish death and suffering on the border. Our focus is strictly humanitarian assistance.

Kino Border Initiative

The Kino Border Initiative's mission is to promote humane, just, and workable migration through: Direct humanitarian assistance and holistic accompaniment of migrants; Education and encounter between migrants and others that transform people and communities toward solidarity with migrants; and Policy advocacy in Mexico and the U.S.

Loretto Sisters

Founded in 1812, the Sisters of Loretto are Catholic women whose pioneering American spirit urges us to answer God's call to live out our baptism by sharing community, our faith, and ministries. We freely choose to radically embrace the gospel of Jesus through the proclamation of three public vows: poverty, chastity (celibacy), and obedience.

Loretto Community members work for justice and act for peace in the United States, at the United Nations, and around the world, including in education, healthcare, spiritual accompaniment, the empowerment of women, environmental stewardship, anti-discrimination, land acknowledgement, and advocacy. Our priority concerns are immigration justice, care for Earth, and the abolition of nuclear weapons.

Maryknoll Sisters

The Maryknoll Sisters is a Catholic organization that believes "that we are all part of One Earth Community... that all of us, regardless of race, nationality, gender, background or personal identity, are all connected as a human family, with each other and with all creation.

We give witness to God's love and devote our lives in service overseas. As nurses, doctors, teachers, theologians, social workers, environmentalists, and more, we serve the needs of the poor, the ailing, and the marginalized throughout the world." There are currently 280 Sisters serving 19 places.

No More Deaths—No Más Muertos

The mission of No More Deaths is to end death and suffering in the Mexico–U.S. borderlands through civil initiative: people of conscience working openly and in community to uphold fundamental human rights. Our work embraces the Faith-Based Principles for Immigration Reform and focuses on the following themes:

- Direct aid that extends the right to provide humanitarian assistance
- Witnessing and responding
- Consciousness raising
- Global movement building
- Encouraging humane immigration policy

Salvavision

Salvavision is a Tucson, Arizona-based nonprofit organization focusing on providing aid and support to asylum seekers, migrants, and returnees. Directed by Dora Rodriguez.

Samaritanos sin Fronteras

Samaritanos Sin Fronteras provides humanitarian aid to migrant shelters in Sonoyta, Sonora, Mexico, while respecting the dignity and autonomy of the shelters. We cooperate and work with all other humanitarian organizations in the area.

School of Americas Watch

School of Americas (SOA) Watch began in 1990 to denounce and bring attention to the 1989 massacre at the University of Central America (UCA) in El Salvador. The Salvadoran military personnel leading the murderous assault were trained at SOA, Fort Moore (formerly Fort Benning), Columbus, Georgia.

SOA Watch is a nonviolent grassroots movement working to close the SOA/WHINSEC and similar centers that train state actors such as the military, law enforcement, and Border Patrol. We strive to expose, denounce, and end U.S. militarization, oppressive U.S. policies, and other forms of state violence in the Americas. We act in solidarity with organizations and movements working for justice and peace throughout the Americas.

In 2016, SOA Watch moved to Nogales, Arizona/Sonora, to call attention to militarized U.S. foreign policy as a principal root cause of migration, as well as the devastating impact U.S. security and immigration policy has on refugees, asylum seekers, and immigrant families all over the continent.

Southwest Center, University of Arizona

A research unit of the College of Social and Behavioral Sciences of the University of Arizona, the Southwest Center has a threefold mission: to sponsor and facilitate research on the Greater Southwest, to publish exemplary work growing from that research, and to act in service to citizens of the region through programs of teaching and outreach. In all three areas, special emphasis is given to strengthening individual and institutional ties to our colleagues at universities and cultural centers in the Republic of Mexico.

Tom Kiefer

Tom Kiefer's ongoing project "El Sueño Americano / The American Dream" centers on photographs of objects confiscated from migrants and asylum seekers at a U.S. Customs and Border Protection processing facility near Ajo, Arizona. Kiefer recovered the items while working there part-time as a janitor and groundskeeper.

The migrants' belongings, necessary for hygiene, comfort, and survival, were deemed "non-essential" or "potentially lethal." Kiefer commemorates the untold stories these objects embody in photographs akin to portraits, preserving traces of human journeys cut short.

Tucson Samaritans

Tucson Samaritans provide water, food, first aid, and other essential items to migrants who cross the border in southern Arizona. Our goal is to alleviate the suffering of people who are making the arduous journey to a better life across the harsh Sonoran Desert. Tucson Samaritans is a grassroots, volunteer-run, humanitarian aid organization.

Veterans for Peace

Veterans for Peace is a global organization of military Veterans and allies whose collective efforts are to build a culture of peace by using our experiences and lifting our voices. We inform the public of the true causes of war and the enormous costs of wars, with an obligation to heal the wounds of war. Our network comprises over 140 chapters worldwide, whose work includes educating the public, advocating for the dismantling of the war economy, providing services that assist veterans and war victims, and, most significantly, working to end all wars.

Vote Common Good

Vote Common Good is inspiring, energizing, and mobilizing people of faith to make the common good their voting criteria. And, we train and support candidates to connect with Evangelical and Catholic voters.

Witness at the Border

We monitor the border, deportation, and detention.

Suggested Reading

A Stranger at My Door:
Finding My Humanity on the U.S./Mexico Border
by Peg Bowden

Against the Wall: My Journey from
Border Patrol Agent to Immigrant Rights Activist
by Jenn Budd

The Line Becomes a River
by Francisco Cantu

The Tortilla Star
by Abbey Carpenter

The Land of Open Graves:
Living and Dying on the Migrant Trail
by Jason de León

Blood Lines: The True Story of a Drug Cartel,
the FBI, and the Battle for a Horse-racing Dynasty
by Melissa Del Bosque

Sand and Blood:
America's Stealth War on the Mexico Border,
by John Carlos Frey

The Distance Between Us
by Reyna Grande

Build Bridges, Not Walls:
A Journey to a World without Borders
by Todd Miller

Crossing the Line:
Finding America in the Borderlands
by Sarah Towle

The Case for Open Borders
by John Washington

The Dispossessed: A Story of Asylum
and the US-Mexico Border and Beyond
 by John Washington

Solito: A Memoir
by Javier Zamora

Glossary

Asylum, Refugee, Migrant

Asylum is a form of protection for people present in the United States who have suffered persecution or fear they will suffer persecution based on race, religion, nationality, political opinion, or membership in a particular social group.

Refugees are people outside their country who cannot return due to the same types of persecution. A person may seek a referral for refugee status only from outside the United States.

A migrant is someone who moves to another place in search of work or better living conditions. An immigrant is someone who moves to a foreign country permanently.

Asylum: Credible Fear Interview

A credible fear interview determines if there is a "significant possibility" that a person can establish eligibility for asylum based on fear of persecution related to race, religion, nationality, political opinion, or membership in a particular social group (USCIS).

Many Latin American migrants flee life-threatening conditions like poverty and violence, but unless they face persecution under the legal definition, they may not qualify for asylum.

Biographic Data

Personal information used to identify an individual, such as name, address, gender, marital status, and date of birth.

Cartel

In the context of Mexico, a cartel is a criminal organization involved in drug trafficking and human smuggling. Cartels now control routes for smuggling migrants and asylum seekers across the U.S.–Mexico border, using complex physical and digital infrastructures.

CBP One Application

A free mobile app launched in October 2020 by U.S. Customs and Border Protection. It allows asylum seekers to submit information and schedule appointments at designated ports of entry along the U.S.–Mexico border. **CBP.gov**

CBP One Application: Issues

The app has faced ongoing problems. In 2023, the CBP undertook a major overhaul of the application following complaints about ongoing issues. However, the issues remain unresolved. There are widespread, documented reports of applicants receiving "system error" messages when the app opens at 9:00 a.m., and at 9:01 a.m., being unable to register. Advocacy organizations and journalists have also reported ongoing problems with facial recognition software failing to detect darker skin tones, raising concerns of racial bias. Despite these issues, the Biden Administration has made CBP One a key part of its border management policy.

Coyote, Guide, Smuggler

"Coyote" is a common term for someone who smuggles migrants across the Mexico–U.S. border. Migrants pay coyotes to guide them, often through dangerous and illegal routes.

Deferred Action for Childhood Arrivals (DACA)

Announced in 2012, DACA allows certain undocumented individuals who arrived in the U.S. as children to apply for deferred deportation and work authorization for renewable two-year periods. DACA does not grant lawful status (USCIS).

Family Reunification Parole

This program allows certain U.S. residents who filed an approved I-130 petition to request parole for eligible family members from Colombia, Cuba, Ecuador, El Salvador, Guatemala, Haiti, or Honduras. It supports safe migration and helps maintain family unity (USCIS).

Human Right to Safety

Everyone has the right to the highest attainable standard of protection against natural and human-made hazards. This right is part of international human rights agreements.

Humanitarian Parole

A discretionary measure that allows someone otherwise inadmissible to enter the U.S. temporarily for urgent humanitarian reasons or significant public benefit (INA section 212(d)(5)). In some cases, such as with Ukrainians and Venezuelans, parole has been granted for up to two years. Approval is discretionary and case-by-case.

Lateral Deportation

A Border Patrol practice of returning migrants or asylum seekers to parts of Mexico far from where they crossed. This often leads to hardship, danger, and the loss of essential items like mobile phones needed for CBP One appointments.

Prevention Through Deterrence

A 1994 U.S. Border Patrol strategy was designed to funnel migrants through remote areas, where harsh environments would deter crossing. This policy has caused thousands of deaths, particularly in the Arizona desert, and increased reliance on smugglers. It remains the dominant border enforcement approach (Undocumented Migrant Project).

Remain in Mexico: Migrant Protection Protocols (MPP)

Started in 2019 and reinstated in 2021, this program requires asylum seekers to wait in Mexico while their claims are processed in the U.S. It has exposed migrants to violence and denied them access to legal protection, while agencies implementing it have faced little accountability (Human Rights Watch).

Sanctuary Movement

A faith-based and political effort that began in the 1980s to shelter Central American refugees fleeing violence. It also called for changes in U.S. foreign policy and encouraged communities to offer protection.

Temporary Protected Status (TPS)

TPS may be granted to nationals of designated countries where conditions, like armed conflict, environmental disasters, or extraordinary events, make it unsafe to return. As of 2025, countries with TPS include Afghanistan, Burma (Myanmar), Cameroon, El Salvador, Ethiopia, Haiti, Honduras, Nepal, Nicaragua, Somalia, South Sudan, Sudan, Syria, Ukraine, Venezuela, and Yemen (USCIS).

Title 42

A public health law used during the COVID-19 pandemic to rapidly expel migrants without due process, denying many the opportunity to seek asylum. Title 42 was enacted under the CDC during the Trump Administration in March 2020 and continued under President Biden until May 2023. Although framed as a public health measure during the COVID-19 pandemic, it was widely criticized as a tool to restrict access to asylum.

Violence Against Women Act (VAWA)

VAWA funds responses to domestic and sexual violence. It also supports undocumented victims of crimes through U visas, which allow them to stay and work in the U.S. if they cooperate with law enforcement. After three years, they may apply for permanent residency (National Network to End Domestic Violence).

Discussion Questions

This isn't just Dora's story, it's for all who carry pain, purpose, and the courage to keep showing up. These questions are meant to spark reflection, connection, and meaningful conversation, whether you're reading on your own, with friends, or in a group. Sit with these stories and explore them together.

Which part of Dora's journey impacted you most deeply, and why? *Were there moments that shifted the way you think about migration or survival?*

How does Dora's story reframe the narrative around people seeking asylum or crossing the desert? *What assumptions did it challenge?*

Dora writes openly about feeling like she never fully belonged in the United States. *How does this sense of in-between identity shape her perspective and her work?*

What does this memoir teach us about bearing witness and when silence becomes complicity? *How does Dora model courage in speaking out?*

How did this book leave you feeling, and what will you carry forward from it? *What are you inspired to do, say, or learn more about?*

If you could ask Dora one question after reading this book, what would it be?

Meet the Authors

Dora Rodriguez is a living symbol of resilience. Through public speaking, grassroots organizing, and hands-on humanitarian work, she educates communities and pushes for transformative change to the inhumane policies and practices along our borders. Dora is the Founder and Director of Salvavision, a nonprofit that provides shelter, aid, and dignity to thousands of migrants and deportees. A proud mother of five and grandmother, Dora lives in Tucson with her husband, and continues to inspire generations with her tireless compassion, courage, and conviction.

Abbey Carpenter is a writer, educator, and advocate for social and environmental justice. Raised in the American West, she holds an M.A. in Sustainable Community Development and has worked extensively in movements focused on equity and ecological resilience. Her debut novel, *The Tortilla Star*, was published by Black Rose Writing, and her work has appeared in *Muse It Up, Sustainable Ways*, and *Read It Here*. Abbey splits her time between Silver City, NM and Ajo, AZ - places that continue to inspire her writing and humanitarian efforts. As she collaborated on Dora's memoir, they discovered the powerful bond of friendship between two women serving with compassion in the borderlands.

---

instagram @dora.luz.rodriguez • *website* / **www.dorarodriguez.org**
media / *speaking engagments* / **anna@dorarodriguez.org**